CAMBRIDGE M   et

Tchaikovsky: Symphony No. 6 (*Pathétique*)

CAMBRIDGE MUSIC HANDBOOKS

GENERAL EDITOR Julian Rushton

Tchaikovsky: Symphony No. 6
(*Pathétique*)

Timothy L. Jackson

The College of Music
The University of North Texas

PUBLISHED BY THE PRESS SYNDICATE OF THE UNIVERSITY OF CAMBRIDGE
The Pitt Building, Trumpington Street, Cambridge CB2 1RP, United Kingdom

CAMBRIDGE UNIVERSITY PRESS
The Edinburgh Building, Cambridge CB2 2RU, UK   http://www.cup.cam.ac.uk
40 West 20th Street, New York, NY 10011-4211, USA   http://www.cup.org
10 Stamford Road, Oakleigh, Melbourne 3166, Australia

First published 1999

Printed in the United Kingdom at the University Press, Cambridge

Typeset in Ehrhardt MT 10½/13, in QuarkXPress™   [SE]

A catalogue record for this book is available from the British Library

Library of Congress cataloguing in publication data
Jackson, Timothy L.
Tchaikovsky, Symphony No. 6 (*Pathétique*) / Timothy L. Jackson.
p.   cm. – (Cambridge music handbooks)
Includes bibliographical references and index.
ISBN 0 521 64111 X (hardback). – ISBN 0 521 64676 6 (paperback)
1. Tchaikovsky, Peter Ilich, 1840–1893. Symphonies, no. 6, op.
74, B minor.   I. Title.   II. Series.
ML410.C4J33   1999
784.2′184–dc21   9839930   CIP

ISBN 0 521 64111 X hardback
ISBN 0 521 64676 6 paperback

For Derrick Puffett, *in memoriam*

Every lover is a warrior; in his great kingdom
Love certainly has his militia too.
When in his prime, with strength to bear
The grievous weight of sword and shield, a man
Will also in love's sieges prove his mettle.
Nor is it undignified to see
Age-palsied hands wielding the sword and lance
Or to hear the grey-beard sigh with love . . .
Who, if not those who follow Venus' flag
Or that of Mars beneath the dark night sky,
Will thus endure the rain, the snow, the wind?
Keep silence, then, O lying tongues, and never
Call love slothful or lascivious,
For love is only for the warrior heart.

Ottavio Rinuccini, from Monteverdi's
Madrigali Guerrieri et Amorosi

Was there, I asked myself, something in the woman's outward appearance that might explain the fundamental condition of her relations with Adrian, the invisibility, the avoidance, the rule that they should never set eyes on each other? She might be ugly, lame, crippled, disfigured by a skin ailment. I do not so interpret it: but rather think that if some blemish existed it lay in the realm of the spirit and taught her to understand every sort of need for consideration and scrupulous tact. Adrian never once sought to break that law; he silently acquiesced in the bounds set to the relationship within the realms of intellect and spirit . . .

The *Lamentation*, that is – and what we have here is an abiding, inexhaustibly accentuated lament of the most painfully *Ecce-homo* kind – the *Lamentation* is expression itself; one may state boldly that all expressivism is really lament; just as music, so soon as it is conscious of itself as expression at the beginning of its modern history, becomes lament and "*lasciatemi morire*," the lament of Ariadne, to the softly echoing plaintive song of nymphs. It does not lack significance that the . . . cantata is stylistically so strongly and unmistakably linked with the seventeenth century and Monteverdi . . . A lament of such gigantic dimensions is, I say, of necessity an expressive work, a work of expression, and therewith it is a work of liberation; just as the earlier music, to which it links itself across the centuries, sought to be a liberation of expression . . .

Purely orchestral is the end: a symphonic adagio, into which the chorus of lament, opening powerfully after the inferno-galop, gradually passes over – it is, as it were, the reverse of the "Ode to Joy," the negative, equally a work of genius, of that transition of the symphony into vocal jubilation. It is the revocation.

Thomas Mann, *Doctor Faustus*
(trans. H. T. Lowe-Porter [Harmondsworth: Penguin Books,
1968, repr. 1974], pp. 378 and 466)

Contents

Plates

Preface

The ideology of the last symphonic utterance as a pessimistic anti–Ninth is deeply rooted in the *Angst* of the last decades of the nineteenth century. Ludwig Wittgenstein aptly described Bruckner's last symphony, his Ninth, as a "protest" against Beethoven's, while Felix Weingartner spoke of Brahms's last symphony, the Fourth, as an "orgy of destruction, a terrible counterpart to the paroxysm of joy at the end of Beethoven's last symphony." But in Tchaikovsky's final symphonic utterance, the *Pathétique*, the ideology of "revocation" assumes a startling new form in a despairing homo–erotic narrative. If the concluding *Adagio lamentoso* lodges its "protest" with Monteverdiesque sighs – "*lasciatemi morire*" (like Adrian Leverkühn's *Lamentation*) – the third movement, the March as the climax of the symphony, boldly explores another aspect of the Baroque amorous *topos*: its military and battle imagery. The *Pathétique*'s novel connection between pessimistic and military discourses represents triumphant homosexual love brutally undercut and punished.

There is no structure without ideology. Metaphorically, structure is intimately connected with ideology; perhaps even born of it. Thus, the belief that one can study "pure" structure, divorced from considerations of the structure's attendant ideology, seems misplaced. I do not posit that "pure" structure cannot be investigated independently, but rather that, because structure is inextricably linked to ideology, investigations of structure must take ideology fully into account. By investigating the ideology of gender and sexuality and – to a lesser extent – race and nationalism, the "new" musicology has raised awareness of these important aspects of ideology. In this book and my 1995 study of "Aspects of Sexuality and Structure in the Later Symphonies of Tchaikovsky," I have attempted to inform rigorous structural analysis with consideration of the relevant ideological, semantic, and semiotic issues.

In discussing the impact of homosexuality, gender, or race upon music, it is important to focus upon the deep structure in addition to levels nearer the musical surface. In the case of Tchaikovsky, this is because his ideology of his homosexuality – in its full complexity – finds its metaphorical reflection in his use of musical language at a deep structural level. More specifically, Tchaikovsky's conception of his "homosexual problem" resonates *metaphorically* rather than literally in his "deviant" backgrounds and other technical aspects of his music. In the following pages, this metaphorical correlation is explored by combining structural analysis with consideration of Tchaikovsky's late nineteenth-century homosexual ideology.

In the course of this study, I shall introduce a number of new concepts. Perhaps the most important of these is the hypothesis of the meta-symphonic narrative, or the contention that a continuous narrative strand extends through a composer's works in a single genre, especially through a sequence of symphonies. Concomitant to this hypothesis is the proposal that the structures of these sequential works in the same genre participate in a larger, overarching structure; from a Schenkerian perspective, the backgrounds (*Ursätze*) of individual symphonies participate in a single largest-scale, overarching background (or meta-*Ursatz*).[1] In this book, I shall propose that structure and ideologies of gender, sexual orientation, and race interrelate and intertwine within meta-symphonic discourses running through the last three Tchaikovsky symphonies, all of the Rakhmaninov symphonies and Symphonic Dances, and the Mahler Symphonies Nos. 5–10. Although demonstration would take us beyond the confines of this study, I believe that the concept (of the meta-symphonic narrative) possesses considerable explanative power for the symphonies of other late nineteenth- and twentieth-century composers.

In writing this book, I benefited from Thomas Kohlhase's new edition (1993) of the *Pathétique*; unfortunately, the critical apparatus for this edition had not yet appeared at the time of writing. When the critical

---

[1] See also my studies of the meta-*Ursatz* in Sibelius: "The Meta-*Ursatz*, Crystallization, and Entropy in the Orchestral Music of Jean Sibelius"; "'A Heart of Ice': Crystallization in Sibelius's *Pohjola's Daughter* and Other Works," *Conference Report of the Second International Sibelius Conference in Helsinki, November 1995*, ed. Veijo Murtomäki, Kari Kilpeläinen and Risto Väisänen (Helsinki: Sibelius Academy, 1998), pp. 247–270.

report is published, one expects that it will contain new information on many matters, most notably regarding the changes that Mengelberg transcribed in his score – presumably in 1897 – falsely believing these to be Tchaikovsky's last thoughts on the piece. Also, it is to be expected that Tchaikovsky's programmatic comments will be accurately transcribed: on p. 70 of his conducting score, Mengelberg made a note concerning the composer's remarks on the cover of his score: "See the back cover page in his score – which *his brother Modest Tchaik.* lent me – [there] are the words of *P. Tchaik* by the horn solo: 'oh, how I love you, oh, my love!!' (etc.) and then again more Russian text."[2] Also helpful were the facsimile editions of the sketchbook and full score (full details are given in the bibliography).

The late Derrick Puffett suggested that I write this book "for him." Not only did Derrick inspire the book, he assisted me in winning the Grant to College Teachers from the National Endowment of the Humanities (1997-98), which enabled me to write it. Thus, this study becomes my grateful tribute to his memory. I would like to thank Joseph C. Kraus (University of Nebraska at Lincoln), William Colson (Southwestern Baptist Theological Seminary), Paul L. Althouse (Connecticut College), my colleagues J. Michael Cooper and Graham H. Phipps (University of North Texas), and my doctoral student Gregory Straughn for many helpful comments and suggestions. My dear friend Solomon Volkov (New York City) provided invaluable assistance, especially with issues concerning Russian culture and language. I also wish to express my appreciation to the series editor Julian Rushton for his constant encouragement and invaluable criticism, and to Penny Souster, Music Editor at Cambridge University Press, for her unwavering support. Finally, I would like to thank my wife, Debbie Estrin, who has stood by me through all difficulties and never lost faith.

---

[2] Quoted from *Willem Mengelberg, Conductor, Exhibition Catalogue* (The Hague: Haags Gemeentemuseum, 1996), p. 82.

1

"Pathetic" metaphors for sexuality and race, gambling and destiny

Perhaps no musical work remains more shrouded in controversy than the Sixth Symphony of Pyotr Ilyitch Tchaikovsky. With regard to the symphony's intrinsic quality, Tchaikovsky himself had no doubts, placing it at the pinnacle of his achievement. To his brother Anatoly he wrote: "I'm very proud of the symphony, and think it's the best of my works." To Vladimir "Bob" Davidov, the dedicatee, he professed that "I definitely consider it the best and, in particular, the most sincere of all my works. I love it as I have never loved any other of my musical offspring."[1] On 30 October, two days after the St. Petersburg premiere, at which the symphony was accorded a polite, bewildered if not hostile reception, Tchaikovsky reiterated his faith in the work to his publisher Jurgenson: "As far as I myself am concerned, I take more pride in it than in any other of my works."[2] Then, a mere nine days after the premiere of this clearly tragic *Symphonie Pathétique*, the composer was dead.

One of the aspects that has to be taken into account when considering the reception of any work of art or music is the role of the creator's own propaganda about it. In preparation for the premiere, Tchaikovsky let it be known that his new symphony had a program, a "sincere," "autobiographical" program, "highly subjective," which he nevertheless declined to reveal. But surely this "secret" program was not really secret at all: the French title *"Pathétique,"* with its connotation of the "forbidden" *grande passion pathétique* of French opera, the public dedication to Bob, and the composer's provocative reticence as to the programmatic specifics were part of a bold – even audacious – propaganda campaign to reveal *de facto* the putatively "secret" program; it was strategically designed to alert friends and even the wider public that the subject of the new symphony was the composer's "unmentionable" love for Bob. This propagandizing effort ensured the work's posthumous success: the composer's sudden death, putatively by suicide, fortuitously made homosexual passion acceptable; now, the symphonic program could become a homily for the expiation of homosexual "guilt" through suicide.

Was this last symphony a kind of musical suicide note, a personal requiem, as was widely believed after the second, posthumous performance? These questions, raised at the dawn of this century, have continued to exercise modern Tchaikovsky scholarship. Indeed the debate between those scholars who believe that the composer committed suicide as decreed by a "court of honor" of his peers at the School of Jurisprudence (Orlova, Brown, and Holden) and those who maintain that he died naturally from cholera as stated in the official reports (Poznansky, Taruskin, some of the current archivists at Klin, and others) has become especially heated in recent years.[3] In the absence of definitive scientific data – the kind of information which could only be provided by an exhumation and modern scientific investigation of the remains – the cause of Tchaikovsky's death must remain an open question. But even a negative result in tests for traces of poison would not put the question to rest since Tchaikovsky might have committed suicide by deliberately drinking unboiled water. The rumors of suicide – especially the story of the "court of honor" – now have become so much a part of the reception history of the *Pathétique* that they deserve consideration as such.

An analysis of a piece of music is, by nature, a hypothesis. Its *raison d'être* is that it has something new to say, that it illuminates the composition, that it causes it to be perceived in a more profound way than previously. There is no absolute proof for the rectitude of any interpretation. Recognizing the truth of this observation, however, does not amount to an unconditional endorsement of relativism or a surrender to the belief that "anything goes"; nor does it give the "green light" to an interpretative free-for-all. On the contrary, it is an *invitation* to construct sensitive analysis-based interpretation founded upon careful review of "the facts." In addition to being hypothetical, an interpretation of the semantic contents of a work like Tchaikovsky's *Pathétique* is bound to be controversial because of the homosexual dimension. At a time when homosexuality is still outlawed in many parts of the world, when – in spite of great progress toward tolerance – we still have a long way to go to ensure that homosexuals receive fair and proper treatment in society, a book that deals with such issues as homosexuality and race, and their impact upon famous pieces, is bound to touch a nerve. It is important, then, to observe at the outset that although the present interpretation considers Tchaikovsky's homosexuality to be a "negative" force in his spiritual-tonal cosmology, this does not in any way endorse the homophobic position that homosexuality *per se* is wrong or evil. The revisionist view of Tchaikovsky's homosexuality as "unproblematic" has resonated well – perhaps too well – with those who rightly wish to see homosexuals "normalized" in our own society. But however welcome recent portrayals of Tchaikovsky as "happy homosexual" may be today, their historical accuracy remains controversial; most importantly, as I shall attempt to show, this revisionist position is *not* borne out by the music – especially by the Sixth Symphony.

Tchaikovsky's music suggests many things which, when viewed closely from our present vantage point, will make us uncomfortable. For example, the plot of the last opera *Iolanta* (1891) resonates with the idea that the "anomaly" is a "medical condition" requiring a "cure"; there is a substantial body of evidence – both external and internal – that a number of Tchaikovsky's major works, including the last three symphonies, present this fateful "anomaly" as an ultimately terminal condition – as an incurable "disease" – which, in the "autobiographical" Sixth Symphony, culminates in the demise of the homosexual lovers (Tchaikovsky and his nephew). As George L. Mosse observes in *The Creation of Modern Masculinity*:

> Moral sickness and physical sickness were thought to be identical, for moral sickness left its imprint on the body and face, as Oscar Wilde sought to demonstrate so dramatically in *The Picture of Dorian Gray* (1890). The avant-garde, which openly attacked the morals and manners of society, was seen in this light, as were all the others who menaced the settled order of things. Physicians took the initiative in ratifying the equation between morality, health, and sickness, partly because this was expected of them and partly because they themselves gained status as the arbiters of established norms. Physicians lent their medical authority to the creation of the moral and physical stereotype of the outsider, whether it be the so-called racially inferior, emancipated women, Jews, or homosexuals.[4]

In my opinion, we must be prepared to acknowledge that Tchaikovsky's highly negative view of a putatively ideal homosexual relationship is profoundly influenced by this late nineteenth-century

3

ideology of homosexuality as a moral and physical "disease" even if it severely jars our modern sensibilities (I shall discuss the homosexual "sickness" metaphor in Tchaikovsky's last three symphonies in Chapter 4).

Let us not discount the possibility that Tchaikovsky was comfortable with his homosexuality in practice, as the "no-problem" theorists have maintained, problematizing it solely in the realm of art. Additionally, the "problem" camp may well have imposed the message of the music upon the life – and the death. In other words, although the Sixth Symphony does intimate a fatal outcome to the relationship between the composer and his nephew, this program does not *prove* that they applied the symphony's dire message to themselves. The inference of suicide drawn shortly after the first performances of the Sixth Symphony and Tchaikovsky's sudden death under "mysterious" circumstances may be false (but one keeps coming back to the troublesome fact that Tchaikovsky referred to the Sixth Symphony as *"autobiographical"*). I shall propose that, *in the music* at least – and, when all is said and done, it is the music that matters – Tchaikovsky *predicts* that the relationship with Bob will have dire consequences. Whether the lovers are destroyed by others or others become instruments of their own deaths remains undetermined (I hope to show that on one level at least, the music intimates crucifixion). Unequivocally clear, however, is the character of the Sixth Symphony as a tragic *"Eros*-symphony."

In the last decades of the nineteenth century and the first of the twentieth century, artists, writers, and composers began to address "difficult" issues with a directness that was essentially new. Although Tchaikovsky referred to the program of the *Pathétique* (his own title) as "secret," in fact its homo-erotic content was made as explicit as possible by the dedication to Bob, and by many other purely musical factors; and this programmatic substance was tactfully recognized (like the composer's homosexuality itself) by Tchaikovsky's immediate circle and widely suspected by the broader public. During approximately two years of gestation (1891–93), this "not-so-secret" program of the Sixth Symphony evolved into an erotic drama of doomed homosexual love richly adorned with intertextual references to opera, specifically to Wagner's *Tristan*, Bizet's *Carmen*, and Tchaikovsky's own operas, especially the last two, *The Queen of Spades* (1890) and *Iolanta* (1891), and a number of earlier works including the Overture *Romeo and Juliet* in its various incarnations (1869, 1870, and 1880) and ballet *Swan Lake* (1875–76).

The "operatic" character of the symphony was already astutely noted in the review of the premiere by Tchaikovsky's friend, the music critic Hermann Laroche. From 1875 on (after seeing *Carmen* and the *Ring*), Tchaikovsky was profoundly engaged with both Bizet and Wagner – and with the Schopenhauerian ideology that inspires Wagner's art: his music embodies his *intuitive* response to Bizet, Wagner, and Schopenhauer. Tchaikovsky's relationship to Bizet and Wagner was dialectical: toward Bizet and a number of other contemporary French composers (especially Delibes), he was favorably inclined, while his attitude to Wagner remained critical. Tchaikovsky's favorable orientation toward French opera and ballet accords perfectly with the generally Francophile sympathies of Russian culture in the nineteenth century.

Rejecting the efforts of the revisionists to deproblematize Tchaikovsky's *Eros*-symphony, I will propose that Tchaikovsky's love-death *topos* (as in Wagner's *Tristan*) – which is realized in a number of other works spanning his career – concerns unbridgeable disjunctions: between the unorthodox (read "homosexual") and orthodox (read "heterosexual") worlds, between the demands of love on the one hand and morality, society, and religion on the other.[5] I will further argue that both the Sixth Symphony and *Iolanta* constitute interrelated tropes on *Tristan*, proposing antipodal yet mutually illuminating solutions to the *Tristan* dilemma. If remaining critical of Wagner, Tchaikovsky himself nevertheless acknowledged Wagner's profound influence, remarking that "I admit I might have composed differently had Wagner never existed" (an admission with which Brahms too could have sympathized). As in *Tristan*, the overall *Eros*-narrative in the *Pathétique* plays out the lovers' unbearable longing springing from their forced separation, their ecstatic union, and their deaths, which are compelled by Destiny in view of the impossibility of their homosexual-"incestuous" relationship from religious, social, moral, and – as I shall argue – (Platonic) philosophical standpoints.

When the nineteenth century approached the "difficult" topics of homosexuality, racism, and religious bigotry in tragic, high art, these issues were generally addressed metaphorically. (For a long time, such topics had been more directly ridiculed in comic, low art.) Nineteenth-century artists and composers enciphered their serious treatment of these issues in a semiotic code, which was tacitly understood by performers and public alike. In the course of the twentieth century we have become accustomed to discussing these "difficult" topics more openly, and are therefore less familiar with the code; this study attempts to break the code and play the game in the late nineteenth-century way. The fundamental yet unwritten rule was that "unacceptable" topics not be aired too openly in high art; rather, considered from a semiotic perspective, the unacceptable signified was better dressed up as a legitimate signifier; thus, homosexuals could historicize themselves, sporting Classical Greek garb in idyllic antique décor, and Jews were free to cloak themselves as "exotic" Gypsies, Huguenots, or Brahmins. Perhaps the first engagement in high art with the "difficult" issues of homosexuality and race occurred in France, where homosexuality had been somewhat fashionable since the later eighteenth century and Jews, emancipated by Napoleon in the early 1800s, had suddenly entered mainstream society.

Armed with the algorithms of this semiotic code, we can begin to probe more deeply the "troubling" aspects of Tchaikovsky's construction of his fate-decreed homosexuality in his music. Those who seek to confine the homosexual aspect to surface structure in Tchaikovsky are barking up the wrong tree; rather, homosexual composers rooted in the Western tradition were not inclined to express their issues in superficialities; these masters created their tragic high art through provocative engagement with their own "fateful" sexual, racial, religious, and gambling "vices" at a much more profound level of musical discourse, this *engagement* (in an existential sense) tending to be deep structural and metaphorical rather than solely lexical in nature.

Tchaikovsky's choice of the French title "*Pathétique*" for his last symphony strategically sights the work in the topical field of French opera rather than Beethoven's Sonata Op. 13.[6] Although Beethoven's symphonic music provided an important formal model for Tchaikovsky's symphonies (see Chapter 3), French music was much more to his taste (as he said in a letter to Nadezhda von Meck, he feared Beethoven as he feared God, but did not love him).[7] The French title squarely places the *Pathétique* in the tradition of grand opera's *engagement* with "difficult" relationships; in this tradition, "forbidden" *grande passion* was frequently interracial, namely between a "white" European and a woman of racially "dubious" origins, the tragic *dénouement* generally resulting in the suicide of one or both lovers.[8] Bizet's *Carmen* (1875), Tchaikovsky's favorite contemporary opera, participates in French opera's treatment of "problematic" – i.e. *pathétique* – interracial relationships. One of Carmen's antecedents is the Black Selika in Meyerbeer's *L'Africaine* (1865), while her Indian and Japanese successors are Lakmé in Delibes's opera of that title (1883), and Cio-Cio-San in Puccini's *Madame Butterfly* (1904, an Italian opera profoundly indebted to this essentially French tradition).[9]

In the last three operas, Passion tempts and ultimately provokes Destiny by daring to cross racial boundaries: the racially "inferior" woman becomes involved in a "forbidden" relationship with a white man; and when he inevitably discards her for the white woman, she commits suicide. In Tchaikovsky's semiotic game of substituting heterosexual for homosexual signifiers, the *"Pathétique"* of French operatic interracial passion becomes his own homosexual passion: in his "Impassioned Symphony" (the French title being crucial to this revaluation) – the *homosexually* stigmatized relationship is substituted for the *racially* stigmatized relationships of French opera. That this transmutation was immediately recognized is revealed by reception history: when composers of the next generation "received" Tchaikovsky's *Pathétique*, they "resolved" its homosexual passion back to the heterosexual but interracial model of the French operatic tradition. Thus, this reconstructed interracial French metaphor informs Mahler's Tchaikovsky-influenced "meta-symphonic" discourse in his last five symphonies, which explore his interracial relationship with Alma. Berg's "passionate" cry to his *Jewish amoureuse* Hanna Fuchs-Robettin in the *Largo desolato* of his *Lyric Suite* (indebted to the *Pathétique*'s *Adagio lamentoso*) similarly refers to the French tradition through a poem which Baudelaire had originally addressed to *la Vénus noire*, the mulatto actress Jeanne Duval.

This fundamental parallelism between the semantic languages of the homosexual composer Tchaikovsky and nineteenth-century French-Jewish opera composers like Halévy, Bizet, and Meyerbeer provides an important key to the semiotic code of the *Pathétique*: just as Tchaikovsky encoded and thereby disguised homosexual messages in the ostensibly heterosexual plots of his operas, ballets, and overtures, these "French" composers employed a related process of reflexive transmutation, trans-

7

forming the persecuted self into a redeemed if not ennobled Other.[10] Since depicting the predicament of the contemporary Jew was too uncomfortable, "French" composers systematically metamorphosed themselves into the eternally fascinating, "exotic" (rather than dangerous) Gypsies, Blacks, and even (in strongly Catholic countries like France and Austria) Protestants.[11] Experiencing the predicament of the French Jew first-hand (being himself half-Jewish), Bizet, his wife (daughter of Jacques Francois Halévy), and her cousin Ludovic Halévy (one of the librettists for *Carmen*) could relate sympathetically to the "Gypsy" Carmen in light of this complex and certainly not unequivocal process of self-transmutation.

French painting at the beginning of the nineteenth century demonstrated astonishing boldness in representing homosexual love. For instance, in the work of Jacques Louis David (1748–1825) and his students, one of whom, Jean Broc, depicted Apollo supporting his mortally wounded youthful lover Hyacinth with surprisingly explicit homoerotic *pathos* (see Plate 1).[12] Even in "liberal" France, homosexual artists and composers were never *legally* allowed out of the closet; it was prudent to hide their issues behind elaborate metaphorical cloaks. Most important for any consideration of the role of homosexuality in nineteenth-century high art-music is to recognize that this century did not even possess a proper, non-pejorative term for homosexuality. The value judgments inherent in nineteenth-century terminology bespeak a conceptual framework in which homosexuality could only be considered negatively.[13] The value-neutral designation "homosexual," invented by the Viennese Karoly Maria Benkert, was not even in use until the turn of the century (i.e. after Tchaikovsky's death). According to conventional nineteenth-century wisdom, homosexuals, Jews, Blacks, Gypsies, compulsive gamblers, and prostitutes all had one essential thing in common: all were criminals teetering precariously on the edge of "proper" society.

Although he had achieved international recognition, Tchaikovsky was keenly sensitive to the ultimate precariousness of his social position; his anxiety finds clear expression in his letters and – I believe – his music. As David Greenberg observes in his monumental study *The Construction of Homosexuality*, "[in the nineteenth century] on the whole, homosexuality was still considered a monstrous vice."[14] Additionally, prostitution (both hetero- and homosexual) and gambling were widely considered to

Plate 1 Jean Broc, *Death of Hyacincth*, 1801

be related and avoidable "vices." In houses of ill repute, the two generally went hand in hand. The centrality of the gambling-with-Fate metaphor in *Carmen* and the ingenious way it is realized musically is also of
great importance for the development of Tchaikovsky's musical thinking. The heroine commands the cards to reveal her future and, although
she is resigned to their dire pronouncement, her questioning *per se* nev-

9

ertheless constitutes a form of gambling, i.e. it is an attempt to cheat Fate by learning the outcome of events before they transpire. For this impertinence (perhaps more than for interracial promiscuity or disloyalty) the sentence is death.[15]

The seminal idea of *Carmen* – "gambling with Destiny" – is taken up by Tchaikovsky in *The Queen of Spades* and the *Pathétique*. In these works, the protagonists audaciously challenge Destiny – to a game whether of cards or of "forbidden" homosexual love makes little difference – which they (falsely) believe is stacked in their favor. By indulging in the associated "vices" of gambling and "forbidden" sex, and by attempting to circumvent Destiny, Fate's bluff is called; its response is death: to "stack the deck," Fate intervenes in the process of "shuffling," thereby tricking and destroying the lovers. As I shall attempt to show, this fundamental idea of Fate's "double-cross" (pun intended) is composed into the deep structure of the music of *Carmen*, *The Queen of Spades*, and the *Pathétique* in a number of dimensions, most strikingly through the metaphor of the "tricked" or "broken" sequences in the tonal and formal domains. There are indications that Tchaikovsky associated the putatively "sinful" compulsions of gambling with homosexuality since in the Kamenka Diary of 1884 the references to them seem to be linked.[16] Since Tchaikovsky was both a compulsive vint player and an active homosexual, his feelings about his homosexual urges may have been intimately connected with his emotions at cards. In *The Queen of Spades*, he subtly associates the "vices" of homosexuality with gambling: the "good" girl Lisa offers herself to Hermann, who misogynistically renounces her to run off to the gambling house.

Many writers have rightly called attention to the centrality of the concept of Fate (*Fatum*) in Tchaikovsky's work. In this book, this contention is supported by a new *aperçu*, namely that the concept of malevolent Fate is worked into the structure of Tchaikovsky's *Pathétique* (and other related works) in two dimensions: firstly, through the use of tritonally "broken" sequences of fifths, and secondly, by means of formal disruptions created by "diachronic transformations" (to be defined shortly). The sequence of descending or ascending perfect fifths becomes a metaphor for the inexorable unfolding of Destiny since one link in the chain "predetermines" the next, the "circle" of fifths paralleling in the tonal domain the turning "wheel" of Fortune. If the circle of fifths unfolds diatonically from C, it "stumbles" upon the tritone B–F, which the theorists designated "the devil in music" ("diabolus in musica"). I shall argue that, in Tchaikovsky and his most important model – Bizet's *Carmen* – the sequence of perfect fifths may be "broken" or "challenged" by the tritone and by sequences of tritones which, drawing upon the tritone's diabolical connotations, represent "difficult" aspects of sexuality and race.

The second trilogy of Tchaikovsky symphonies can be understood to participate in a "Meta-Symphony" or meta-symphonic discourse. There is a clear line of demarcation between the first and last three numbered symphonies; the earlier works are "Russian" or "abstract" in character, while the later symphonies are closely related testimonials of a personal and self-revelatory nature (as we have seen, Tchaikovsky himself referred to his Sixth Symphony as "autobiographical" and "highly subjective"). The Fourth Symphony can be said to mark the "turning point" or "crisis" in Tchaikovsky's career as a symphonist, initiating the large-scale, meta-symphonic narrative concerning the "anomaly." In this narrative spanning Symphonies Nos. 4–6, the Sixth Symphony becomes the *dénouement*.

To support this interpretation of the Sixth Symphony, the book analyzes the *Pathétique* in the larger context of the meta-symphonic discourse spanning Symphonies Nos. 4–6, Tchaikovsky's oeuvre as a whole, and European music at the turn of the century. This contextualization will enable us to decode and disentangle the complex web of semantic meanings woven into the symphony's tonal and formal fabric. The second chapter presents the historical background for the *Pathétique*'s genesis and composition, placing it in the context of Tchaikovsky's biography and creative activities in the early 1890s. The third chapter provides a detailed formal and tonal analysis, which orients the reader for the detailed exposé of the putatively "secret" program in the fourth chapter. Since sketch study is most illuminating *after* a work has been thoroughly analyzed, the investigation of the sketches and short score for the Sixth Symphony is postponed until Chapter 5; now the examination of the work's compositional genesis in the sketchbook can be illuminated by interpretative insights gleaned in earlier chapters. The sixth chapter focuses on the reception of this innovative work. Shortly after its second performance, the *Pathétique* enjoyed huge

11

success throughout Europe and America, perhaps not least because of the whiff of scandal associated with the composer's death. It quickly became a "landmark" of Western music, and exercised a considerable influence on composers of the next generation, most notably Mahler, but also Rakhmaninov, Berg, and possibly Sibelius and Britten. It is noteworthy that, in a Nazi revaluation, the *Pathétique* enjoyed new popularity in the late thirties, the March becoming an allegory for the resurgence of the "New Germany," and the concluding *Adagio lamentoso* a *Heldenklage*. The book concludes by considering the account of the Court of Judgement purely as reception history and the parallels it evokes between Tchaikovsky and Plato's Socrates, who was similarly accused of "corrupting youth," condemned by an Athenian court, and forced to commit suicide. The parallelism with Socrates suggested by the story of the secret judgement reinforces the interpretation of Tchaikovsky's masterpiece as a hymn to the Platonic conception of love as a form of divine, yet fatal madness.

2

Background and early reception

It seems likely that Tchaikovsky began thinking about the program of the Sixth Symphony in 1891, and that it evolved and was modified as the work took shape in 1893. The initial idea was for a study of "Life," but this more abstract, generalized program metamorphosed into a highly personal yet idealized account of the composer's relationship with Bob. Aspects of the history of this "grande passion" were also portrayed in the cycle of songs to texts by Daniil Rathaus (Op. 73). The song-cycle, conceived at approximately the same time as the symphony, is closely related to the *Pathétique*.

That the Sixth Symphony was composed with a specific program in mind was confirmed by the composer. As I have already observed, the mere act of "unmentioning" the unmentionable was – *per se* – a bold, even audacious, propaganda strategy. In a letter to Bob (11 February 1893) penned during composition of the work, Tchaikovsky reported (as explicitly as possible):

> While on my travels I had an idea for another symphony – a program work this time, but its program will remain a mystery to everyone – let them guess. But the symphony will be called "Program Symphony" (no. 6). . . This program is imbued with subjectivity. During my journey, while composing it in my thoughts, I often wept a great deal.[1]

There has been some confusion whether the title "*Pathétique*" originated with Tchaikovsky or was invented by the composer's brother Modest and then sanctioned by Pyotr. Modest asserted that he had come up with it the day after the St. Petersburg premiere on 16 October 1893. But this claim is neither borne out by the facts nor consistent with the work's "non-secret" program. The reference to the symphony as the "*Paticheskaya simfoniya*" in an unpublished letter to Tchaikovsky from the publisher Pyotr Jurgenson dated 20 September opens up the possibility that it was *Tchaikovsky* – not Modest – who had already decided to subtitle the symphony "*Paticheskaya simfoniya*" *before* the premiere, although the composer employed the French translation "*Symphonie Pathétique*" on the title page of the manuscript.[2] This chronology is vitally important because it suggests that Tchaikovsky wished to identify the work as an *Eros*-symphony from an earlier point in the compositional genesis. (Exactly when in the compositional process Tchaikovsky settled on the title "*Pathétique*" remains unknown.)

The precise relationship between the program for a "Life" Symphony, the so-called "Seventh" Symphony (i.e. the aborted E♭ Major Symphony), and the program for the Sixth Symphony remains complicated and unclear. The known facts may be quickly recapitulated. On the return voyage from America in May 1891, Tchaikovsky began sketching a symphony in E♭ major. In the same sketchbook containing sketches for the new symphony, he also drafted a program:

> The underlying essence . . . of the symphony is *Life*. First part – all impulsive passion, confidence, thirst for activity. Must be short (the Finale death – result of collapse). Second part love: third disappointments; fourth ends dying away (also short).[3]

A year later, in the spring and summer of 1892, Tchaikovsky apparently was again at work on the E♭ Major Symphony. On 13 July of that year, he reported to the composer Taneyev: "In May I sketched the first movement and Finale of a symphony." In September, he told the pianist A. Siloti: "The outline is ready, I am now working on the score. What manner of symphony it is that I have written, by God I do not know . . . I dream of finishing the score in December . . ."[4] By 4 November, the sketches for the entire symphony were complete. Then, quite suddenly, Tchaikovsky became very critical of the new symphony; on 28 December, he wrote to Bob complaining that "it was written less from any 'creative need' than 'purely for the sake of writing something.' There's nothing at all interesting or sympathetic in the entire piece. I've decided to put it aside and forget it."[5] Apparently, Tchaikovsky had already written out the full score of the E♭ Major Symphony, but then destroyed it. However, he did not abandon the musical content; instead, he used the sketches to convert this symphony into the Piano Concerto No. 3 in E♭

Op. 75, the Scherzo-fantasie Op. 72, No. 10, and the Andante and Finale for Piano and Orchestra Op. 79 (incomplete). In a letter to the composer Ippolitov-Ivanov from 24 March 1893, Tchaikovsky refers to this compositional transformation: "I do not know whether I told you I had a symphony ready, but tore it up, as I took a sudden dislike to it. Now I have . . . composed a new symphony, *which I shall definitely not tear up*. I have also sketched out a piano concerto . . ."[6] The sketches for the E♭ Major Symphony survived and were used by S. Bogatyrev in 1951–55 to reconstruct it.

Tchaikovsky scholars generally agree that the "Life" program entered into the sketchbook containing the E♭ Major Symphony sketches is both contemporaneous with and related to the E♭ Symphony, and that when Tchaikovsky abandoned this symphony, he transferred its program to the Sixth Symphony. Poznansky asserts that "the program in question [i.e. the program of the Sixth Symphony] is no mystery at all. In fact, Tchaikovsky developed the composition to a great extent from the sketches for an earlier work, a symphony in E♭ major (1891–92) which he planned to entitle *Life* in his notebooks, but which he considered a failure and never completed."[7] Holden takes essentially the same view: "In this [i.e. the program of the "Life" Symphony] we can recognize the outlines of the program for what turned out to be the *Pathétique*."[8] Joseph C. Kraus concurs: "His first attempt at realizing his intentions [for the "Life" Symphony] was the unfinished Symphony in E♭ Major, sketched in autumn of 1892 but eventually reworked as the Third Piano Concerto Op. 75, the Andante and Finale Op. 79, and the Scherzo-fantasie Op. 72, No. 10."[9]

There is, however, a serious problem with this widely believed hypothesis, namely that the *music* of the E♭ Major Symphony as outlined in the sketches appears to be incompletely related to the "Life" scenario and to the music of the Sixth Symphony. Therefore I do not subscribe to Poznansky's hypothesis that Tchaikovsky developed the Sixth Symphony from the sketches for the E♭ Major Symphony. Furthermore, the conclusion of the "life" program is not realized in the E♭ Symphony: the Finale of the E♭ Symphony, which is of substantial proportions in the sketches (321 measures long in Bogatyrev's realization), ends triumphantly. It is certainly not "dying away" as stipulated in the "Life" program. With its mention of "death," "collapse," and "disappointment," the "Life" program is clearly tragic, while the E♭ Major Symphony is a cheerful, vivacious, relatively untroubled work from start to finish. Perhaps the "Life" program was to be realized in another unspecified work, which Tchaikovsky temporarily abandoned and which later in 1893 evolved into the Sixth Symphony. And perhaps it was with reference to this as yet unrealized program that Tchaikovsky wrote in the same sketchbook: "Why? Why? To what end?"

If the "Life" program was not fully realized in the aborted E♭ Major Symphony, it does seem to have formed the basis of the program of the Sixth Symphony. Although the *Pathétique*'s first movement is not "short," one can recognize in the restless, agitated materials the "Life" program's "impulsive passion, confidence, thirst for activity." The program's characterization of the second movement as "love" accords – in the final version of the symphony – with the second movement, and also with the second subjects of the first and last movements. It is impossible to hear "disappointments" in the third movement, which projects a mood of defiant energy rather than defeat; rather, this idea was shifted to the Finale: in the concluding movement, one can clearly discern the program's projection of "the Finale *death* – result of collapse" and "ends dying away (also short)," which has been amalgamated with the projected third movement's "disappointments."

Genesis and early reception

The Sixth Symphony was sketched between 16 February and 5 April and scored between 1 and 31 August 1893.[10] While working on the Sixth Symphony, after completing its March but before sketching its Finale and second movement, Tchaikovsky seems to have encountered a compositional block. Like many other composers in similar situations, Tchaikovsky occupied himself with other, less arduous projects: he made an arrangement of the B♭ episode from Mozart's Fantasia in C Minor K. 475 for vocal quartet and piano (completed 13–15 March) and, if Polina Vaidman's hypothesis concerning a draft in the Sixth Symphony sketchbook is correct (see Chapter 5), he also may have begun to compose a cello concerto-type piece, which Vaidman suggests was to be a "Concert Piece for Cello and Orchestra"; this piece was then abandoned when the composer returned to the Sixth Symphony to compose its Finale and Waltz. I shall propose that Tchaikovsky overcame his compositional block by transforming his initial idea for the first of the Op. 73 Romances, "We Sat Together" (conceived in August 1892) into the B section of the *Pathétique*'s Finale. Between sketching and orchestrating the Sixth Symphony (i.e. during the summer months of 1893), Tchaikovsky produced the Eighteen Pieces for Piano Op. 72 (composed 19 April–3 May), finished the Six Romances Op. 73 (written out 5–17 May), converted the first movement of the E♭ Major Symphony into the Third Piano Concerto Op. 75 (arranged 5–13 July), and began arranging a separate Andante and Finale for Piano and Orchestra Op. 79 from material intended for the later movements of the E♭ Major Symphony (unfinished, and orchestrated by Taneyev).

In October 1893, Tchaikovsky returned to the Sixth Symphony to prepare and revise both the orchestral score and the piano duet transcription for performance and publication. At this point, the composer sought the assistance of two instrumentalist friends: Jules Konyus, the violinist, advised him on bowings, while his brother Lev, the pianist, critiqued Tchaikovsky's arrangement for piano duet. On 20 October, Taneyev and Lev performed the piano reduction at Taneyev's house with the young Sergei Rakhmaninov among the invited guests. The next day, the Moscow Conservatoire's student orchestra read through the score to facilitate correction of the orchestral parts. The much-anticipated premiere was given in St. Petersburg on 28 October.

It is noteworthy that these first performances of the symphony repelled early listeners. Jules Konyus later reported: "I must confess that I was really not in the least attracted by the actual music of the Sixth Symphony since the author's performance was as bad as one may imagine. His red hands with thick and by no means supple fingers pounded out the most poignant passages crudely and hurriedly, as if they hastened to finish and rid themselves of that boring thing."[11] According to Tchaikovsky's young composer friend Ippolitov-Ivanov, who was present at the 20 October performance of the piano reduction, "the symphony did not make much impression on us." At the premiere, the symphony was also accorded a negative reception, the critic Hermann Laroche (while admiring the symphony himself) admitting that audience reaction was ambivalent if not hostile: "If they did not get to the core of Tchaikovsky's Sixth Symphony today, then tomorrow or the day after tomorrow they will begin to appreciate it and, in the end, come to love it."[12]

Only at the second performance on 6 November, that is after Tchaikovsky's death, was the *Pathétique* acclaimed a masterpiece. Perhaps the work's content had been made acceptable by the composer's death, once it was widely suspected that, unable to bear his homosexuality any longer, he had committed suicide. In other words, only when Tchaikovsky could be comfortably pegged as an "*un*happy" homosexual," and the *Pathétique* interpreted as a self-indictment (i.e. as his own pronouncement through his music that the "right" and "proper" solution to his "homosexual problem" was suicide) – only then could the *Pathétique* become morally acceptable. Thus, Tchaikovsky's putatively self-inflicted punishment of suicide "cleansed" both himself and the symphony, enabling the *Pathétique* to become widely accepted.

This interpretation of the *Pathétique* as self-indictment and personal requiem, which has persisted until our own day, is not entirely without basis in the music; the requiem interpretation is supported by the quotation of the Russian Orthodox Requiem in the first movement. Because of this quotation (and, of course, on account of the many other programmatic elements to be discussed), the symphony quickly became a death-symbol for Russians. In his memoirs concerning Tchaikovsky, Georges Balanchine addresses this issue:

> And then comes the burial hymn "Repose the Soul." . . . Only people from the past, like me, understand what that really means: that "Repose the Soul" is sung only when someone has died. A bier stands in the church, the coffin lid is open, and when the service is coming to an end, everyone kneels and weeps: this man is *dead*! "Repose the soul of your deceased servant with the saints." It's more than an *Ave Maria* or *Ave Verum*. This begs the saints up in heaven to grant peace to the soul of the deceased. Tchaikovsky wrote that about himself! There's a whirlwind flying through it, a whirlwind! And then down, down, the horns with oboes and bassoons. And suddenly: "Repose the soul." Everybody's crying.
>
> And in the Finale of the *Pathétique* there is a soft, otherworldly chorale – three trombones and a tuba. The melody goes down, down, dies out: strings, then woodwinds. Everything stops, as if a man is going into the grave. Going . . . going . . . gone. The end. Tchaikovsky had written his own requiem![13]

Robert Craft reports that, as Stravinsky lay dying, he tactlessly put on a recording of the *Pathétique* in the next room and was reproved by Madame Stravinsky: "Now at the sound of the first movement, V[era] runs into the room, begs me to turn it off, says that to Russians it predicts death."[14]

To counter the notion that Tchaikovsky was depressed and suicidal in the last year of his life, Poznansky cites as a *coup de grâce* a letter from the composer to the young Russian law student Daniil Rathaus dated 1 August 1893. Rathaus was the amateur poet who had provided the texts for Tchaikovsky's last set of songs, the Six Romances Op. 73. In this letter, the composer seems at pains to reassure the young man that, in spite of the "sad" character of his settings, he is generally a "happy person:"

> In my music I claim utter candour, and although I too have a predilection for songs of wistful sadness, yet, in recent years at least, I, like yourself, do not suffer from want and can in general consider myself a happy person![15]

However, this statement is not unequivocal. On the one hand, Tchaikovsky posits the "utter candour" of his melancholy music, while on the other he confirms that he is a "happy person." Wherein does this happiness lie? In this statement, at least, Tchaikovsky seems to associate "happiness" with newly won financial independence and material comfort, rather than with his inner life. According to Poznansky, "none of these [last] pieces seems particularly tragic . . . the songs after poems by Daniil Rathaus, even though not devoid of some passionate melancholy, do not strike one as at all morbidly pessimistic."[16] But a closer examination of the song-cycle fails to confirm Poznansky's assessment.

While recognizing the dangers of extrapolating from art to biography, I am struck, nonetheless, by the unmistakable connections between Tchaikovsky's life and art, not only with regard to the *Pathétique*, but also his last original composition, the Six Romances comprising the Op. 73 song-cycle – a work which I believe to be intimately associated with the *Pathétique* both in subject matter and genesis (I shall discuss the programmatic and genetic connections in more detail in Chapters 4 and 5). These songs – clearly arranged into a cycle – also represent a "pathetic" *grande passion* in which the lovers, long separated, desperately yearn for one another; they finally are able to meet to enjoy a single night of bliss only to be cruelly parted once more, this time probably forever. One of the central problems of Tchaikovsky's relationship with Bob was the frequent separations necessitated by the composer's obligations as a celebrity – and also by the need for discretion – and this distress is expressed in his letters, the symphony, and the song-cycle. Without doubt, the anguish of living apart is the overriding theme in these songs. But – *pace* Poznansky – the cycle *is* profoundly "pessimistic," even "morbidly" so. The first two songs – which may be related to the *Pathétique*'s Finale (see Chapter 5) – are characterized by the despairing phrase (in Song 1) "And now I am once more alone, / and expect nothing from the future." If these songs can be taken to be semantic keys to the *Adagio lamentoso* – as I believe they must (for motivic reasons to be discussed below) – the outcome of the symphony is indeed "pessimistic." Does the cycle succeed in moving beyond the tragedy depicted in the Symphony's Finale to intimate the protagonist's acceptance of the situation and his transfiguration through spiritual embodiment of the beloved (as is suggested in the fifth song)? I think not; rather, the tragic fade-out in the last song (which parallels the *diminuendo al niente* at the end of the *Pathétique*) interprets the poem's potentially equivocal final lines not simply as "resigned benediction" but also as "final *adieux*": "My dear friend, pray for me, / As I am always praying for you."

This programmatic connection between the tragic *grande passion* portrayed in the Six Romances and the *Pathétique* is supported by compositional chronology. It is a matter of not inconsiderable interest that Tchaikovsky should have decided to set a group of poems sent to him by an unknown law student "out of the blue" in August 1892. I suspect that he was powerfully attracted to their contents because they spoke to him fortuitously and "with utter candour" of the drama with Bob being played out in his inner life; in view of this connection, he decided to set them immediately upon receipt, and began sketching the first song "We Sat Together" and the fourth "The Sun Has Set" at that time. But the project was not to be completed quickly; these settings would not be dashed off in the heat of the moment (as were some of Tchaikovsky's other works); rather, perhaps in view of their great personal significance, they were allowed to coalesce slowly for almost a year before being set down on paper in the first two weeks of May 1893. In other words, the cycle was germinating during precisely the same period in which the

Sixth Symphony was being conceived and drafted. Thus, in terms of their compositional genesis, and musical and poetic content, the Six Romances are intimately connected with the *Pathétique*; I shall discuss this interrelationship more fully in Chapters 4 and 5.

3

Form and large-scale harmony

According to common wisdom, Tchaikovsky's greatest weakness was form; Laroche already articulated widespread opinion when he complained: "It appears that he [Tchaikovsky] was able to cope with all other technical difficulties, but mastery of form persistently eluded him" – a view that has been restated many times in the literature.[1] Tchaikovsky himself acknowledged a "lack of continuity in the sequence of separate episodes." Perhaps, when comparing their music with that of their "Classical" predecessors, a number of late nineteenth-century composers rightly worried that their music was insufficiently "organic." The ideal of the Classical sonata had been dynamism: through harmonic motion coupled with subtle motivic relatedness and transformation the music powerfully created the associated effects of goal-oriented forward motion and organic unity. But in the hands of later nineteenth- and early twentieth-century composers (Tchaikovsky, Bruckner, Strauss, Mahler) sonata form ran the risk of stultifying in excessively stable and self-contained thematic-harmonic units. Perhaps this general tendency toward formal sectionalization combined with harmonic stasis resulted from composers learning sonata form from theorists' codifications in *Formenlehre* treatises instead of from living tradition. And perhaps with some justification, some composers like Tchaikovsky (Bruckner also comes to mind) were right to complain that their "seams showed," i.e. that their music was a succession of good ideas clumsily or neatly, in Tchaikovsky's case, patched together as opposed to an organic whole.

But the assertion that Tchaikovsky's music is formally unsophisticated, or awkwardly confined in conventional formal-tonal straitjackets, is simply not borne out by careful analysis. On the contrary, the music exhibits remarkable innovation, freedom, and imagination in its treatment of form. Furthermore, it is precisely in the area of form that innovative works like the *Manfred* Symphony and the *Pathétique* were most influential on the next generation (especially on Mahler and Rakhmaninov). Tchaikovsky recognized the innovative aspects of design and structure of his last symphony, not only in terms of his own symphonic oeuvre but in the larger context of the symphonic repertoire as a whole. In a letter to Bob, he observed: "There will be much that is new in this symphony where form is concerned, one point being that the Finale will not be a loud allegro, but the reverse, a most unhurried adagio."[2]

Before considering the unusual form of the *Pathétique* in greater detail, it is helpful to contextualize its formal innovations by reviewing the conventions of symphonic form, sonata form, and the formal structures of Tchaikovsky's preceding symphonies. To explain the *Pathétique*'s form, it is necessary to recognize that "normative" formal categories operate on three levels: (1) on the "global" level of a group of interrelated symphonies, i.e. the "meta-symphony" comprising the interrelated Symphonies Nos. 4–6, (2) the "macro"-level of the individual symphony as a whole, and (3) on the "micro"-level of the individual symphonic movement. "Normative" macro-symphonic form defines the four-movement disposition of the symphony as standardized in the later symphonies of Mozart, and especially the earlier Beethoven symphonies. Normative sonata form is defined by common practice of late eighteenth- and early nineteenth-century composers (especially late Haydn and Mozart, and Beethoven) and codified by mid-nineteenth-century theorists (e.g. Marx, Lobe). One might argue that, isolated as a Russian composer, Tchaikovsky remained "out of touch" with this mainstream European tradition and that his music cannot be measured against the yardstick of "normative" symphonic and sonata forms as defined by German-speaking composers and theorists. But both the biographical facts and the internal evidence of the music speak loudly against this conclusion: through his training and travels, especially in Germany, Tchaikovsky constantly kept in touch with important musical developments in central Europe; additionally (as we shall see shortly), his music conforms in large measure to the formal categories codified by the German-speaking composers and theorists. In spite of his partiality for French opera (discussed earlier), Tchaikovsky's orientation in formal matters was clearly German, this German influence probably originating in his early training under the Germanophile theorist Nicholas

Zaremba and pianist-composer Anton Rubinstein at the St. Petersburg Conservatory.

In many nineteenth-century symphonies, both the macro-symphonic form and/or the individual micro-sonata form may play out the strife-to-victory "redemption" paradigm, also described as *per aspera ad astra* ("through adversity to the stars"). The strife-to-victory narrative may incorporate within itself a battle *topos*, whereby military imagery may assume spiritual and amorous connotations (cf., for example, the discussion of the March in Chapter 4). Within the symphony as a whole, the large-scale harmonic plan may realize the *ad astra* narrative through the victory of the major over the minor mode in the Finale. In this case, the macro-symphonic structure is "end-weighted," the underlying compositional idea being to defer the achievement of redemption until the Finale, or until the last possible moment in the musical discourse, i.e. until the Finale's coda. Tchaikovsky's First, Second, Fourth, Fifth, and *Manfred* Symphonies conform to this model. Similarly, within the minor-mode sonata form of the individual movement, victory may be represented by the triumph of the major mode in the recapitulation. The first movements of Tchaikovsky's First and Second Symphonies attempt but fail to achieve this kind of modal victory.

To facilitate discussion of form, I shall follow the conventions of twentieth-century analytical parlance. In normative sonata form, the groups in the exposition occupy "exposition space"; the corresponding groups in the recapitulation occupy "recapitulation space." The introduction, development, and coda each occupy their own respective "spaces." Generally speaking, both introduction and coda spaces remain extraneous to the sonata space proper. The exposition and recapitulation "spaces" are generally divided into a first group and second group, and sometimes a closing group. In recent work, a number of scholars have begun to investigate the way in which Tchaikovsky and his contemporaries transformed, "deformed," and "re-formed" the normative sonata form paradigm.[3] There are various types of "deformations." Within the individual sonata form, these include harmonic procedures conflicting with the normative harmonic patterns of sonata form and unusual formal dispositions, which generally affect the recapitulation. For example, the recapitulation might be cut or truncated in various ways, or it might be reversed or partially reversed. Additionally, new material could be introduced unexpectedly into the sonata form, a technique which has been described as break-through (or "Durchbruch"). Let us consider Tchaikovsky's use of these deformations.

"Truncated" sonata form may be realized by omitting the recapitulation of the first group; in this case, the role of reprise is assumed entirely by the second group. The second version of the Finale of Tchaikovsky's Second Symphony provides a clear example of the "truncated" reprise: revising the symphony in 1879–80, Tchaikovsky eliminated the recapitulation of the first group. The effect of this cut is that the recapitulation in the final version is reduced to the second group (mm. 513–651), which leads directly to the coda (m. 652–end). In "reversed" sonata form, the groups are recapitulated in reversed order so that the second group rather than the first initiates recapitulation space. While Tchaikovsky does not employ the reversed recapitulation in his symphonic works, he does use a type of "partially reversed" recapitulation in which the first theme of the first group is superimposed upon the end of the development and thus occurs within development space (it also marks the climax of the development). The anticipated recapitulation of the first group is then "interrupted" by the recapitulation of the second group, which initiates recapitulation space (as in reversed sonata form). In view of this displacement, the coda takes on the assignment of realizing the previously "interrupted" first group's recapitulation.[4]

The term "Durchbruch" was coined by Paul Bekker to describe the sudden, unexpected arrival on D major at the end of the development in the first movement of Mahler's First Symphony (mm. 352–57). Adorno, Hepokoski, and others have generalized Bekker's "Durchbruch" as an event which (in Hepokoski's words), "sunder[s] the piece's immanent logic."[5] The break-through may involve the unexpected presentation of new thematic material anywhere in the sonata form, although it generally occurs in the development or recapitulation rather than the exposition. But if the break-through takes place in the exposition, its material stands outside the sonata form proper and is never recapitulated in the normal way.[6] In terms of the *ad astra* redemption paradigm, the break-through may be an epiphanal revelation of the redemptive state to be definitively experienced at the end of the spiritual pilgrimage.

Super-sonata form and macro-symphonic diachronic transformation

Normative macro-symphonic form may be defined as the four-movement form generally employed in the later symphonies of Haydn and Mozart, and in those of Beethoven. The first movement, usually in a faster tempo, is in sonata form. The second movement is in a slower tempo, while the third movement is either a Minuet with Trio or a Scherzo. The Finale, usually in a fast tempo, can be in either rondo or sonata form. Tchaikovsky's Symphonies Nos. 1, 2, 4, and 5 conform to this four-movement macro-symphonic paradigm. The Third Symphony achieves its five-movement disposition by interpolating the "Alla tedesca" as an "extra" movement between first movement and the "Andante." Not only are the first five symphonies essentially traditional in their macro-symphonic formal disposition, each concludes with a triumphant Finale fulfilling the *ad astra* metaphor (although one might question the sincerity of the triumphs depicted in the Finales of the Fourth and Fifth symphonies).

For programmatic reasons, Tchaikovsky deforms normative macro-symphonic form in *Manfred* and the *Pathétique*; the forms of these symphonies are Tchaikovsky's most complicated macro-symphonic deformations. The technique of synthesizing individual movements of a composition within a single, unified sonata form, first explored by Beethoven in his last works and further developed by Liszt in his tone poems and piano sonata, had a profound effect on later nineteenth-century composers, including Tchaikovsky. I shall refer to this kind of synthesis as "super-sonata symphonic form." In super-sonata form (sometimes called a "sonata-in-one"), the three spatial divisions of sonata form – exposition, development, and recapitulation – are superimposed upon the design of a unified – usually (but not always) continuous – four-movement macro-symphonic form. In this superposition, the first movement generally fills the exposition space containing the first and second groups of a normative sonata form, and the Finale is assigned to recapitulation space and encompasses the recapitulation of the first and second groups. The spatial envelope of either "development space" or "recapitulatory space" is then extended by interpolating spatial envelopes for the other movements, usually a slow movement

26

and Scherzo, into the spatial envelope of the development or recapitulation.

Manfred's "disquiet" and "restlessness" are programmatically composed into the *Manfred* Symphony's large–scale formal dislocations. In the first movement, the sonata form's development space is eliminated, the exposition (mm. 1–288) being immediately followed by the recapitulation (mm. 289–end). Within the exposition, the massive first group presenting Manfred's motives (mm. 1–170) is followed by the second group associated with Astarte (mm. 171–288). The first movement's displaced development space is "restlessly" "bumped up" ("exiled," like Manfred himself) to the next level of spatial organization, namely the macro–symphonic form. At this next (macro–symphonic) level, the Scherzo and Andante (second and third movements) occupy development space. Thus, the formal displacement of the development in the first movement converts the symphony's normative four-movement macro–symphonic form into a super-sonata symphonic form encompassing the entire symphony: the first movement occupies exposition space, the Scherzo and Andante development space, and the Finale recapitulation space.[7]

In later years, Tchaikovsky became dissatisfied with the *Manfred* Symphony as a whole (although he still believed in the first movement's intrinsic quality). Perhaps a weakness of *Manfred*'s super-sonata symphonic form is the (programmatically?) "fitful" sectionalization it imposes upon the Finale, the major formal units tending to be separated by rests, which destroy continuity. One could argue that, in the *Pathétique*, Tchaikovsky sought to recompose certain elements of the *Manfred* Symphony, especially its programmatic macro–symphonic deformations; yet this time he achieved that elegant simplicity of expression which he felt had eluded him in the earlier work. This may account for the many significant parallels between the *Manfred* Symphony and the *Pathétique*. Most notably, both are tragic symphonies in B minor, both are program symphonies dealing with "forbidden" liaisons (the *Manfred* Symphony representing the tragic consequences of Manfred's incestuous union with his sister Astarte, the Sixth Symphony the homosexual relationship of the composer with his nephew), and both can be understood as super-sonata symphonic forms in which the outer movements function as exposition and recapitulation and the interior movements occupy development space. In the Sixth, this super-sonata effect is realized more subtly than in *Manfred*: whereas in the earlier symphony, the Finale relies upon thematic reprise from the first movement to achieve the super-sonata form, in the Finale of the Sixth, there is no recapitulation from the first movement; instead, the Finale more subtly creates the effect of symphonic super-sonata form by recomposing the first movement's large-scale harmonic structure (as we shall see, its $\hat{3}$–$\hat{5}$–$\hat{1}$ auxiliary cadence).

Elsewhere, I have proposed a theory of diachronic transformation that is related to Saussure's concept of "diachronic" linguistic transformation, observing that

> Saussure's distinction between synchronic and diachronic "facts of a different order" can illuminate the entelechy of musical structure . . . A musical work may embody in its endstate a conceptually prior state, which has become the endstate through a diachronic transformation. From a synchronic perspective, the endstate is a "distortion" of the previous state and vice-versa . . . Diachronic transformation ruptures a steady state to create a duality of previous state and endstate and, from a single synchronic perspective, distortion and paradox.[8]

Drawing upon this theory of "diachronic transformation," I posit a conceptually "previous" formal state of the *Pathétique*'s macro-symphonic form, which is "distorted" in the work's "endstate." Essentially, I propose that, in its conceptually earlier state, the symphony conforms to normative macro-symphonic form (articulated in Symphonies Nos. 4–5) by concluding with a March-Finale and fulfilling the *per aspera ad astra* redemption narrative. Then, in a diachronic transformation designed to undercut the *ad astra* narrative, the slow movement is shifted from an interior position and transformed into the Adagio Finale, the March thereby being converted from a triumphant Finale into the third movement. Within the "global" "meta-symphonic" discourse spanning Symphonies Nos. 4–6, the Fourth and Fifth Symphonies both conform to and establish the macro-symphonic norm; but in the "endstate" of the *Pathétique*, the slow movement, shifted from its proper place *prior* to the March, tragically concludes both the symphony and the meta-symphony.[9] In the annotations in the sketchbook, Tchaikovsky refers to the third movement as both a Scherzo and a March. This terminology notwithstanding, the March is certainly not a traditional Scherzo either in form or substance. But Tchaikovsky does not abandon the traditional Scherzo idea; rather, in the spirit of super-sonata symphonic concept, he amalgamates the Scherzo with the first movement by assigning its character and spatial mass to the first group and bridge in the first movement's exposition (mm. 22–88).

To summarize, in the *Pathétique* the normative four-movement macro-symphonic paradigm experiences expansion, synthesis, and diachronic transformation. In its "endstate," the first movement conflates a Scherzando-fantasy with the opening movement proper. In the "previous state," the defiant March attempts to assert itself as the Finale, but the spatially shifted *Adagio lamentoso* usurps its dramatic role. In the "endstate," the symphony is noteworthy for its treatment of the *ad astra* metaphor: as a residual effect of the "previous state" (lurking in the "background"), the initial three movements play out the *ad astra* narrative, which is fulfilled in the March; but this triumph is then brutally undercut by the *Adagio lamentoso*. For this reason, I shall refer to the overall symphonic narrative as a "failed" *ad astra* metaphor. This capriciously undercut *ad astra* metaphor is closely connected with Tchaikovsky's larger conception of malevolent Fate dramatically intervening in the "endgame" – whether of life or cards or musical form is immaterial – with disastrous results. An essential idea in the *Pathétique* – also clearly formulated in *The Queen of Spades* – is that the protagonists gamble on controlling Destiny; they call Fate's bluff and it responds by cheating. In the final scene of *The Queen of Spades*, for example, just at the point when Hermann thinks he has played the winning ace, Destiny substitutes the Queen of Spades; similarly, in the Sixth Symphony, just in the instance when the March believes it has achieved the *ad astra* narrative, it is undercut by the tragic Finale.

Meta-symphonic connections

The Fourth through Sixth Symphonies are harmonically linked in several dimensions. Firstly, the large-scale F–B tritonality presented so emphatically by the first movement of the Fourth Symphony is also played out by the cornerstone symphonies of the narrative, i.e. by Symphony No. 4 in *F* and No. 6 in *B* – and also within the Sixth Symphony's outer movements as *B–E♯* (cf. the discussion of Appendices A–C in

Chapter 4). Secondly, the E major-minor tonality of the Fifth Symphony concretizes the "fateful" appearances of the E major as "undertonic" to F major-minor in the Fourth Symphony's introduction and Finale (i.e. in the interpolated introduction in the Finale, mm. 199ff.). Finally, the Fifth Symphony is linked to the Sixth through the *Pathétique*'s introduction, which suggests a continuation of the Fifth Symphony's E minor tonality (only subsequent events reveal that B minor rather than E minor is destined to be the tonal center of the *Pathétique*).

First movement

The sonata form of the *Pathétique*'s first movement is innovative in its design-structural coordination. The space normally allocated to the first group is occupied by material which I shall call Scherzando-fantasy. Since a narrative unfolds through the course of the movement (indeed, the symphony as a whole), Tchaikovsky avoids a literal or close recapitulation of the first group; rather, its reprise (mm. 245–67) significantly transforms the Scherzando material to depict novel events in the drama. The structural dominant at the end of the recapitulated first group (mm. 277ff.) supports a new, "Oracle" theme in the trombones, which creates the effect of a break-through.

Considered from a harmonic perspective, the first movement also deforms the traditional harmonic plan of a minor-mode sonata. The remarkable character of the Sixth Symphony's highly unstable opening becomes immediately apparent when compared with the much more conventional openings of Symphonies Nos. 1–5.[10] The introduction (mm. 1–18) suggests a tonic – E minor – but subsequent events soon undermine this impression (the invocation of E minor links the Sixth with the Fifth Symphony). At the beginning of the movement proper, i.e. at the "Allegro non troppo" (mm. 19ff.), the music clearly indicates that B minor is the main key center but a strong, root position B minor tonic is nevertheless withheld (Appendix A, a). The root position B minor tonic chord, which should resolve the first inversion dominant chord at the end of the introduction, is suppressed never to appear; rather, in the opening gesture, the expected root position tonic chord is displaced by a highly unstable first inversion tonic, which immediately moves to an unresolved dominant (m. 19).

Let us continue the harmonic analysis of the first movement, and specifically its first group. Assuming the character of a Scherzo, the first group is highly unusual harmonically. At no point does Tchaikovsky land on a structural tonic chord in root position. The only candidate for a structural tonic might be the B minor root position triad in mm. 36–38, but closer analysis reveals this chord to be passing in nature. In context, it is construed as the "upper fifth" of the preceding E minor chord (in mm. 27–34). Indeed, the Scherzo as a whole beginning on D in m. 26 is controlled by a playfully animated ascending fifth sequence, the B chord being just one link in the chain: D (m. 26) – A (m. 26) – E (m. 27) – B (m. 36) – F♯ (m. 42) – C♯ (m. 50) – G♯ (m. 66), which resolves as a leading tone to A (m. 70). The underlying idea is to arpeggiate the D chord: D (m. 26) – F♯ (m. 42) – A (m. 70). This chord, established in the Scherzando first group, is then prolonged throughout the second group (mm. 89–160).

Although the music has avoided a structural tonic throughout the first movement's introduction and exposition, one might expect it to conform to sonata form convention by articulating a strong structural tonic at the beginning of the recapitulation. But this expectation remains unfulfilled; rather, as at the outset (m. 19), the composer again suppresses a root position tonic at the beginning of the recapitulation (m. 245), landing instead on the first inversion of the B minor tonic chord. By avoiding a root position tonic at this formal-structural juncture, the music "passes through" the expected tonic, prolonging D in the bass from the exposition through the development to the beginning of the recapitulation. The bass then ascends from D to F♯, which is first construed as G♭ (m. 263) and subsequently transformed enharmonically into F♯ (m. 267). The definitive arrival on the tonic, now converted from B minor to major, is delayed until the beginning of the recapitulated second group (mm. 305–34) and the "design" coda (mm. 335–54).[11] In this way, over the course of the first movement in its entirety, the bass realizes a massive enlargement of the auxiliary cadence: D–F♯–B (3̂-5̂-1̂, I⁶–V–I).

The later movements

In his memoirs, Balanchine perceptively calls attention to the *Pathétique*'s unity:

And it's all masterfully, wonderfully connected: the melodies in the Finale resemble the theme in the first movement. And the tonalities are similar. Everything, everything is thought out! It's extraordinarily interesting to follow how it's all done.[12]

An essential compositional idea in the first movement is to take the D major chord established in the Scherzando exposition (mm. 26ff.) and, by exchanging its fifth A with the sixth B above the bass D, to convert the D chord into a B minor tonic six-three at the beginning of the recapitulation (Appendix A, a). To forge subtle links between movements, Tchaikovsky also employs this strategy in the symphony's later movements: it becomes the basis for the large-scale harmonic organization of both the second movement and the Finale (Appendix A, b and d). In the second movement, which is a large-scale ternary form A (mm. 1–56) B (mm. 57–95) A′ (mm. 96–151) plus coda (m. 152–end), the B section in B minor is surrounded by A and A′ sections in D major (Appendix A, b). At no point in the B section, however, does Tchaikovsky allow the music to articulate a stable root position B minor triad; rather, the entire B section extends the B minor chord in six-three position. Clearly, the compositional idea here is to generate the B minor passage by means of exchanging the A of the D chord for B, which then resolves back to A ($\hat{5}$-$\hat{6}$-$\hat{5}$ over D). Tchaikovsky works the same procedure of converting a D major five-three into a B minor six-three in the Finale. In this movement, which is conceived as a strophic binary form A (mm. 1–36) B (mm. 37–81) A′ (mm. 88–146) B′/Coda (mm. 147–end), the B section or second subject greatly extends the D major chord (mm. 37ff., Appendix A, d). At the climax of this passage (mm. 70–71), the D major chord is converted into a B minor six-three chord (*not* a root position five-three chord). This procedure accords with Tchaikovsky's larger harmonic strategy: as in the first movement, he wants to delay the definitive arrival on the B minor tonic in root position until the end of the movement (mm. 147ff.).

The third movement, the March, is a large bipartite structure (as opposed to the normative ternary form of a Scherzo): Part 1 comprises mm. 1–138 and Part 2 mm. 139–end (Appendix A, c). Each of these two large parts is then further subdivided into two sections, with a cadenza between the second A′ and B′ to yield the form: Part 1: AB / Part 2: A′ Cadenza B.′ The first A section is binary: a (mm. 1–34 and mm. 138–72)

– b (mm. 35–70 and mm. 173–94). The role of the A section is introductory, i.e. it foreshadows the presentation of the March theme proper in the second B section. The B section (the March theme in its entirety) is a ternary form: a (mm. 71–96 and mm. 229–54) – b (mm. 97–112 and mm. 255–82) – a′ (mm. 113–38 and mm. 283–end). The extended cadenza (mm. 195–228) leads to the second, final statement of the March.

Armed with this outline of the third movement's form, let us consider its larger harmonic organization (Appendix A, c). The movement as a whole is clearly in G major. At first glance, the music appears to begin on the G major tonic; however, closer examination of the harmonic framework reveals a very curious harmonic twist: at the outset, the initial G chord – the putative tonic – does not really function as the tonic at all but rather is interpreted in context (of the A section, mm. 1–70) as III of E minor. Thus, in the first eight-measure phrase, the harmony presents an auxiliary cadence in E: III (mm. 1–6) – V (m. 7) – I (m. 8). E is then clearly prolonged through its extended dominant (mm. 19–26). The G that underpins the b section (mm. 37ff.) is still heard not as the definitive tonic but rather as III of E minor; it is the middle term of the arpeggiation: E (m. 8) – G (m. 37) – B (m. 61) spanning the A section. In the B section (mm. 71–138), Tchaikovsky employs mixture, moving from E minor to major, the full March theme being presented in E major. In the A′ section, the bass moves again from E (m. 146 = m. 8) to G (m. 175 = m. 37) but instead of continuing up a minor third to B as the dominant of E (as it did in m. 61), it ascends a whole step to A (m. 191), which functions as the supertonic of G. The cadenza's purpose now becomes obvious: its role (mm. 195–228) is to dramatize the cadence into G major and the decisive arrival on the tonic: II (mm. 195–220) – V (mm. 221–28) – I (mm. 229ff.).

Let us return now to the Finale which, of all the later movements, is most closely related to the first. Kinship between the outer movements is established by a number of common features. Harmonically, the primary themes of the first and last movements are interrelated. In the first movement, the main theme (mm. 19–20) articulates the incomplete harmonic progression I^6–V; if the "dysfunctional" seventh chord at the beginning of the Finale is explained as a B minor tonic chord "with added sixth" (G♯) in first inversion, then the overall harmonic progression underlying the Finale's main theme (mm. 1–2) is similarly I^6–V. In the Finale, as in the first movement, this I^6–V harmonic progression is first presented by the opening theme *in nuce* and is then expanded to become the basis of the large-scale harmony. And as in the first movement, the resolution of V to I is provided by the tonic at the return of the B section (mm. 147ff.), which simultaneously functions as a coda. To be sure, one might propose as a candidate for "strong root position tonic" the root position B minor chord in m. 12. But my interpretation of this harmonically complex passage does not accord this B minor chord definitive tonic status; instead, it is construed as a passing harmony. The overall harmonic progression in these measures (mm. 1–18) is I^6 to III (m. 6) to II^6_5 (mm. 16–18): the B minor triad in m. 12 is heard in the context of the passage as a whole as a passing harmony generated from the D chord in m. 6 and interposed between the $\mathrm{D}\,^5_3$ (m. 6) and $\mathrm{E}\,^6_5$ (m. 16) chords.

The III chord (D major) established at the beginning of the B section (m. 37) is converted into a I^6 chord at the climax (m. 71), as noted above. In the larger context of the A and B sections taken together (mm. 1–73), the bass descends through the augmented fourth F♯–C: F♯ (m. 2) – E (m. 30) – D (m. 37)- C♮ (m. 73). Essentially, the tonic six-three articulated in m. 1 moves to the emphatic arrival on the Neapolitan (C) in root position in m. 73. The rushing descending octave scales (mm. 77–80) broken off abruptly by the ascending octave (m. 81) and followed by the rhetorical pause (extended by the *fermata* over the rest) create the impression that the movement might attempt to conclude in the key of C. The transition (mm. 82–89) recomposes – as a "composed-out echo" – the upper voice of the previous passage, the descending octave scale g^2–g^1 (mm. 82–88) now being "answered" by the ascending octave f♯^{1}–f♯^{2} (m. 89). Perhaps one might be tempted to interpret the B minor chord in the transition (m. 84) as a definitive arrival on the tonic, but Tchaikovsky subverts its tonic status by transforming it into a passing chord: in the passage as a whole, the bass ascends by step, A♯ (m. 83) – B (m. 84) – C♯ (m. 87), as the upper voice descends by step, G (m. 83) – F♯ (m. 88). In mm. 88–89, the music regains the I^6, which initiates the reprise (mm. 90ff.). In the larger context of mm. 81–88, then, the bass ascends chromatically from the Neapolitan (C) back to the tonic in first inversion on D: C (m. 81) – C♯ (m. 87) – D (m. 88).

In the recomposition of the A section (mm. 104–46), the Neapolitan again receives tremendous emphasis (i.e. as in mm. 73–81). This time, however, it occurs in six-three position (mm. 115ff.) and functions as a pre-dominant chord. This Neapolitan supports c^4, the "Phrygian" supertonic (B minor: $\flat\hat{2}$) and goal of the upper voice, which collapses stepwise through three octaves to c^1: c^4 (m. 115) – b^3 – a^3 (mm. 116–17) – g^3 – f^3 (m. 118–19) – e^3 – d^3 (mm. 120–21) – $c\sharp^3$ – b^2 (mm. 122–23) – a^2–g^2 (mm. 124–25) – $f\sharp^1$ (mm. 126–34) – e^1 (m. 135) – d^1 (m. 136) – c^1 (m. 139, cf. the discussion of the "registral embrace" metaphor in Chapter 4). The definitive arrival on the tonic (mm. 147ff.) coincides with the definitive resolution of the Phrygian $\flat\hat{2}$ (C) to $\hat{1}$ (B). The entire recomposition of the B section (m. 147) simultaneously functioning as the coda extends the final tonic resolution of the auxiliary progression I^6 (m. 109) – V_4^6 (m. 126) – V_3^5 (m. 146) – I (m. 147).

The unified harmonic structure of the *Pathétique*'s super-sonata form is shaped and conditioned by the auxiliary cadence (Appendix A). In exposition space, the first movement presents the auxiliary cadence D-F♯-B (bracket "a" in Appendix A, a), which becomes paradigmatic for the symphony as a whole; in recapitulation space, the Finale recomposes the D-F♯-B of the first movement (bracket "a" in Appendix A, d). Furthermore, the D of the second movement is regained by the D at the beginning of the fourth movement (see the dotted beam in the example); thus, the D-F♯-B auxiliary cadence can be understood to be expanded over the last three movements. Like the symphony's first and last movements, the March is structured as an auxiliary cadence, the larger harmonic strategy being to withhold the definitive arrival on the tonic (as in movements I and IV) until the end of the movement. The March theme is foreshadowed in the "dark" key of E minor (mm. 1ff.), then played through in the "wrong" key of E major (mm. 71ff.), foreshadowed again in E minor (mm. 139ff.), finally to triumph in the "right" key of G major (mm. 229ff.). This progression from "darkness to light" is realized by means of the auxiliary cadence E–A–D–G (G major: VI–II–V–I), the background sequence of descending fifths (equals ascending fourths) clearly being motivically generated from the foreground fourths in the March theme itself.

4

The "not-so-secret" program – a hypothesis

Since a number of independent contemporary witnesses testified that, according to Tchaikovsky, the "not-so-secret," "withheld" program of the Sixth Symphony had "autobiographical" significance, the generic program – "Life" – clearly experienced a considerable evolution between 1891 and 1893 to become much more focused – "autobiographically" and "subjectively," as Tchaikovsky described it – on a particular life, namely Tchaikovsky's own. Sensing a contradiction between the tragic tone of the putatively autobiographical symphony and the composer's allegedly happy circumstances in 1893, Poznansky asks: "If the Sixth Symphony was indeed intended to be somehow autobiographical, why then was it so pervasively tragic in tone?" He observes that "no truly catastrophic events accompanied Tchaikovsky's final years. He was at the peak of his creative powers, famous, and loved by those whom he loved."[1] Poznansky's solution to this conundrum is two-pronged: to downplay Tchaikovsky's own assertions that the symphony's withheld program was "autobiographical" and to locate the source of the symphony's pathos not in Tchaikovsky's own life or personal circumstances but rather in what he calls Tchaikovsky's (more abstract) "ultimately tragic creativity."[2]

My own view is that, if Tchaikovsky's outer life was "happy" in view of his material comfort and worldly success (as described in the above-cited letter to Rathaus), his *inner life* was considerably more complicated and troubled than Poznansky intimates. I would further posit that the narrative program of the Sixth Symphony *is* intimately related to Tchaikovsky's relationship with Bob Davidov. His sexually "anomalous" love for Bob continued to be "problematic" in the larger context of his personal and social–religious circumstances; this "problem" deserves to be explored sensitively since it underlies various narrative strands in his last works.

Tchaikovsky's homosexuality was tacitly or tactfully recognized in the nineteenth century, posthumously deliberately concealed from the public by his brother Modest and others, and surrounded by a wall of official silence in the Soviet Union (especially during the Stalinist period). But even in the Soviet period, Tchaikovsky's homosexuality was well known and widely discussed. For example, the Shostakovich of *Testimony* observes "Really, we musicians do like to talk about Mussorgsky, in fact I think that it's the second favorite topic after Tchaikovsky's love life."[3] Since the early 1990s, with the Communist collapse and the relative opening up of Russia, the composer's homosexuality has ceased to be an officially taboo subject; on the contrary, many of the previously censored facts in the letters, diaries, and excerpts from Modest's unpublished autobiography now have been widely exposed.

The positions of recent biographers vis-à-vis Tchaikovsky's homosexuality provide the material for an interesting reception history, especially since their views usually bear directly upon their interpretation of the program of the Sixth Symphony and their position in the natural death versus suicide debate. Two main camps can be discerned: the traditionalist "problem" camp, i.e. those who recognize a "homosexual problem" and believe that it was a contributing factor to both the tragic tone of the Sixth Symphony and the composer's alleged suicide (although the one certainly does not predetermine the other), and the revisionist "no-problem" camp, which recognizes neither a "homosexual problem" (post-1878) nor a suicide.

For the "no-problem" camp, the composer's homosexuality became essentially *unproblematic* after the marital crisis of 1877–78. Indeed, the very assertion of a "homosexual problem" is anathema to these commentators; any troubling aspects of the composer's homosexuality were confined to the period of the marriage fiasco.[4] After weathering this storm, Tchaikovsky's happy solution was to love young males in his social class romantically and to gratify his sexual needs among members of the lower class.[5] For the "no-problem" camp, Tchaikovsky's death is completely unconnected with his homosexuality: as officially reported, the composer died naturally from cholera. More importantly for the present study, Poznansky and others do not consider the "homosexual problem" to be a factor in the "secret" program of the *Pathétique*. Holden re-endorses the Orlova–Brown position that Tchaikovsky's homosexuality continued to trouble the composer long after the marriage fiasco, contributing both to the program of the Sixth Symphony and to the composer's putative suicide.

Tchaikovsky engaged in behavior that might be condemned today as that of a pedophile; some of his most significant relationships were with young boys and included middle-class children, as well as male child-prostitutes in the major cities which he visited (Italy – one of Tchaikovsky's favorite haunts – was notorious for its boy prostitutes). Perhaps the pubescent child was particularly attractive precisely because his/her sexuality is not as fully developed or clearly defined as that of the adult person. In late nineteenth-century eyes such boy-girl children possessed the androgynous quality of redeeming angels. Accordingly, the androgynous angelic child was an important *topos* in late nineteenth-century art and literature. As I shall suggest, this idyllic, angelic quality can be discerned in Tchaikovsky's idealizations of his boy-loves in his music. Tchaikovsky's relationships with the young boys such as Eduard Zak and Davidov may have unbalanced them later in life – a not uncommon outcome when children have had sexual relations with adults. Indeed, Tchaikovsky himself harbored concerns in the case of Zak, the fifteen-year-old Conservatory student who in 1869 presumably inspired the love-theme in *Romeo and Juliet*, and who committed suicide four years later. As late as 1887, Tchaikovsky was still anguished about his role in Zak's suicide, confiding to his diary: "My God! No matter what they told me at the time, and how I have since tried to console myself, my guilt about him is unbearable."[6] It is noteworthy that the other great love of Tchaikovsky's life, his nephew Bob, with whom the composer was involved from an early age, shot himself in 1906, aged only thirty-four.

There are indications that later in life Tchaikovsky continued to be troubled by his homosexuality, and certainly by the problematic aspects of his "romantic" love for his nephew Bob. In the eyes of the "proper" society in which Tchaikovsky-the-celebrity moved, the liaison with Bob was, of course, "forbidden," and had to be concealed, not simply as homosexual; it was also incestuous. The composer's homo-erotic passion for Bob dates at least to 1884, when the composer was forty-four and his nephew just thirteen. The summer diary of 1884, which miraculously survived destruction at the end of Tchaikovsky's life, already discloses the composer's powerful passion for Bob.[7] What is exceptional is that Tchaikovsky's passion survived Bob's puberty, and there are many indications that Bob returned the composer's love. That Bob was in Tchaikovsky's immediate family both raised his status (elevating him far above the young boy prostitutes and servants who provided Tchaikovsky with sexual outlets) and provided cover for a long-term intimate association.[8] In his will, Tchaikovsky treated Bob like a wife: it was Bob – not Modest – who would receive the bulk of the royalties and copyrights, and he essentially became the executor of the will, responsible for dividing up the wealth among the heirs. (In 1897, Bob moved to Klin to live with Modest and to help set up a memorial to Pyotr Ilyich.) It was – ironically – perhaps the very *success* of the relationship that led Tchaikovsky's "homosexual problem" to resurface in an even more complicated and intense guise than previously. Bob the boy-Muse grew up to be the youth-Muse and, in this capacity, became an essential part of Tchaikovsky's creative-spiritual existence. But with fame came responsibilities as a world-renowned composer, national hero, and cultural ambassador for Russia; this prominence precluded a more open relationship with the nephew. The "homosexual problem" now became imbued with the "anguish" of the lovers brought about by their need for discretion and their frequent, sometimes lengthy separations forced by Tchaikovsky's professional engagements, i.e. his tours abroad.[9]

Taking up Tchaikovsky's challenge with regard to the Sixth Symphony's program, my own "guess" is that it is a rich tapestry of interrelated narratives all of which contribute to the idea of homosexuality as an incurable "disease" culminating in the destruction of the protagonists – it is for this reason that (to cite Thomas Mann's description of Leverkühn's *Lamentation*, which is clearly modeled on the *Pathétique*) the "symphonic adagio" is the "revocation" of the "Ode to Joy." In the following pages, I shall propose a "new" interpretation of the *Pathétique's* narratives – all united under this concept of "revocation" – the word "new" being placed in quotation marks because I wish to emphasize that the "not-so-secret" program was widely recognized both intuitively and tacitly in the nineteenth and early twentieth centuries. People in the late nineteenth and early twentieth centuries "knew" that Tchaikovsky was a homosexual and those in his inner circle recognized that he had a "special" relationship with his nephew. But because it concerned a taboo matter, i.e. a homosexual-incestuous uncle–nephew relationship, the

Pathétique's program could not be explicitly formulated in words – not even by the composer himself. Nevertheless, the dedication in conjunction with well-recognized musical *topoi* provides the common vocabulary through which Tchaikovsky could encode and his listeners decode the "not-so-secret" program of the Sixth Symphony. My "new-old" reading of the program, then, is based upon a reconstruction of this (encoding/decoding) semantic process informed by the relevant historical and biographical facts.

The *Pathétique* as a tragic *Eros*-symphony is the culmination of different yet interrelated narratives in Tchaikovsky's life's work. All of these varied narratives are united by the "autobiographical" dimension: according to the "plot" of the Sixth Symphony, Tchaikovsky believed that the relationship with Bob was an "illness" which would prove deadly. I shall suggest that this "fatal" aspect derives from two considerations: (1) by obstinately pursuing their "forbidden" love, the lovers "gamble" with Fate, i.e. they call its bluff and Destiny responds by destroying them, and (2) their love proves to be fatal because *Eros*, as a form of divine madness, cannot survive in the phenomenal world.

The seductive male other: idyllic visions of the boy-Muse

A central problem of Tchaikovsky's own statements on programmaticism is that he could not articulate the fact that his last three symphonies are connected with his homosexuality or, more precisely, with his idealizations of his boy loves. This fact must be kept in mind when considering the program for the Fourth Symphony that Tchaikovsky drew up for von Meck.[10] However, his characterization of the second subject of the Fourth Symphony's first movement as a "bright and gracious human form" is remarkably candid:[11]

> Is it not better to turn away from reality and submerge oneself in dreams? O joy! There is at last a sweet and tender dream appearing! A bright and gracious human form flits by and lures us on somewhere. How lovely! And how remote the obsessive first allegro theme now sounds! The dreams have now taken full possession of the soul. All that was gloomy and joyless is forgotten. Here it is, here is happiness![12]

Surely this enticing "human form" is an oblique reference to the type of the young boy prostitute that Tchaikovsky found so enticing during his European wanderings. The music itself – the short licks in the winds – eloquently suggests the "flitting" form, precisely the kind of playful "grace," the angelic quality that Tchaikovsky found so charming in young boys. The program's reference to "happiness" resonates with the description of sexual happiness in a letter to Modest from 26 February 1879, describing a night with a young French boy-prostitute in Paris: "There occurred all kinds of *calinerie* [tenderness] as he put it, and then I turned frantic because of amorous happiness and experienced incredible pleasure. And I can say in confidence, that not only for a long time, but almost never have I felt so happy in this sense as yesterday."[13]

The program's depiction of "a sweet and tender dream appearing! . . . a bright and gracious human form" also accords perfectly with the musical characterization of Bob as a seductive boy- and youth-Muse in the *Pathétique*. In the first movement, the "scherzando" first group portrays Bob as a pubescent boy, while the second group constitutes an idyll depicting idealized love between the composer and Bob as young man and angelic Muse. The portrayal of the beloved as Muse – also as a redeeming angel – and the lover's source of strength and refuge from a turbulent and dangerous world, is a typically nineteenth-century *topos*. Bob is the very incarnation of those qualities that Vaudémont dreams of and Iolanta embodies: "[Love] dreams of an immaculate angel, of a soft and heavenly vision . . . with the look of a cherub stamped with heavenly sweetness, a being from another world, whiter than the snow in spring, purer than the lily of the valley, softer than lilies in the field . . ."[14]

The cheerful, cavorting scherzando-fantasy/first group also recalls images of the youthful Bob recorded in Tchaikovsky's 1884 diary. Then, in the second group's "love music" (mm. 90ff.), Tchaikovsky draws upon a number of musical *topoi* to create the effect of a secluded idyll and paint a languorous portrait of Bob as youth-Muse and "redeeming angel." The long pedal drones on D (mm. 90–95 etc. and mm. 142–60) and the simple harmonic progressions allude to the Baroque *Pastorale*, thereby creating a bucolic effect. The closed form of the second group, A (mm. 90–100) – B (mm. 101–29) – A′ (mm. 130–41) plus Coda (mm. 142–60), also contributes to the impression of a timeless, Arcadian love relationship. Bob is idealized in celestial, hymnal tones. Whereas the descending-scalar motive playfully represents the young Bob in the scherzando first group ('celli and basses, mm. 42–43; flutes, oboes, clarinets, mm. 44–45, etc.), in the second group, the descending-scale arabesques from F♯ (violins and 'celli, mm. 89–100, etc.) depict the graceful, still angelic yet now more mature, introspective, and self-possessed youth.[15]

Punishment for the "sin" of homosexuality: the Last Judgment

An important component of Tchaikovsky's "homosexual problem," which has been ignored or downplayed, is the composer's Christian "anxiety" with regard to his homosexuality. Christianity's implacable hostility to homosexuality informs the closely related Greek and Russian Orthodox traditions (as well as Western Catholicism) according to which homosexuality is a "sin" punishable by eternal perdition. There are strong indications in the last three symphonies that the composer associated this Christian eschatological belief with his pessimistic view of his own homosexuality. Tchaikovsky's religiosity – albeit unorthodox – is indicated by many factors, both biographical and musical. Like many composers, he hoped to be blessed by inspiration from God. Consider, for example, the annotation at the end of the *Particell* sketches for the Sixth Symphony, where Tchaikovsky expressed his gratitude to the Deity for granting him the inspiration to complete the symphony.

Modest reports that at Maidanovo in 1885, Tchaikovsky established a routine of work and study that he was to follow at home for the rest of his life: "Pyotr Ilich got up between seven and eight o'clock. Between eight and nine he drank tea, usually (being an incorrigible smoker) without bread, and read the Bible."[16] As a composer of liturgical music, Tchaikovsky produced a number of choral settings for the Russian Orthodox Church, and authored a brief manual on harmony in Russian religious music.[17] Tchaikovsky's sacred music is heartfelt; in a letter to von Meck, he articulated his religious feelings:

> I attend Mass frequently. The liturgy of St. John Chrysostom is one of the most exalted works of art. Anyone following the liturgy of the Greek Orthodox service attentively, trying to comprehend the meaning of each ceremony, will be stirred to the very depth of his being. I am also very fond of evening prayers. There is nothing like entering an ancient church on a Saturday, standing in the semi-darkness with the scent of incense wafting

through the air, lost in deep contemplation to find an answer to those perennial questions: wherefore, when, whither, and why? Startled out of my pensive mood by the singing of the choir, I abandon myself entirely to the glowing fervor of this enthralling music when the Holy Door opens and the tune "Praise ye the Lord" rings out. This is one of the greatest pleasures in my life.[18]

Although religion continued to play a strong part in Tchaikovsky's life, his faith was far from perfect. As he continued to von Meck:

As you can see, I am still bound to the Church by strong ties, but on the other hand I have long ceased to believe in the dogma . . . This constant inner struggle would be enough to drive me out of my mind were it not for music, that great comforter, the most exquisite gift Heaven has bestowed on mankind living in darkness . . . Music is a loyal friend, a source of strength and solace, something worth living for.[19]

From his extensive reading of the Bible, Tchaikovsky must have known that homosexuality is considered a cardinal sin to be severely punished on the Day of Judgment; Christianity's stern condemnation of homosexuality lurks in the background of the *Pathétique's* narrative: the protagonists have enjoyed a "forbidden," "sinful" love.[20] The pejorative terms available to discuss homosexuality in the nineteenth century (e.g. "perverts") reflect the prevailing Judeo–Christian conception of homosexual behavior as "sinful," an inclination which must be resisted or overcome by an act of will and faith. The plot of *Iolanta* intimates that the "anomaly" – congenital "blindness" – can be "cured" only through religious faith. The idea that this miraculous "cure" was to be effected by faith in God rather than medical science is clearly articulated in the opera's final chorus:

ALL: Glory to the Creator, from whom all good things come.

IOLANTA, THE KING: Receive thanks from your servants, O Lord!

IOLANTA: Before your throne stand the heavenly armies of cherubs. You are merciful, and your love is boundless. You shine in the smallest of your creatures like a ray of sunshine.

ALL: Receive thanks, O Lord. You have allowed the miracle. You have returned her to light. Your love is boundless. You have delivered your servant from the realm of darkness. O Lord, giver of all good things, glory be unto you! Hosanna to the highest! You cause the light of truth to shine out to the Glory of the all-powerful Lord![21]

In October 1893, just after completing the orchestration of the *Pathé-tique*, Tchaikovsky declined Grand Duke Konstantin's suggestion to set a poem entitled "Requiem" by Apukhtin.[22] Tchaikovsky defiantly observed that:

> My latest symphony, just finished and due to be performed . . . is steeped in very much the same spirit as [Apukhtin's] poem *Requiem*. I consider the symphony a success, and hesitate to repeat myself so soon by undertaking a work so similar in spirit and character. There is another reason why I am little inclined to compose music for any sort of requiem . . . In the requiem there is much talk of God the Judge, God the Punisher, God the Avenger(!!!) Forgive me, your highness, but I dare to suggest that I do not believe in such a God – or at least that God cannot stir in me those tears, that rapture, that awe before the creator and source of every good which might inspire me.[23]

But if an artist does not believe in the literal truth of Christian eschatology, nevertheless he may exploit its symbolism and connotations in his work. Tchaikovsky readily acknowledges the parallelism between the *Pathétique* and the Requiem by recognizing the potential redundancy of setting Apukhtin.[24]

Tchaikovsky's statement that he does not believe in and cannot be inspired by God as Judge, Punisher, or Avenger has a shrill ring of defiance that seems most forcefully expressed in the *Pathétique*'s March. However, this bravado is tragically "revoked" by the *Adagio lamentoso*. In light of the references to Christian eschatology in all of the last three symphonies (and especially to the Requiem in the first movement of the *Pathétique*), one cannot escape the impression that Tchaikovsky's homosexual lovers defiantly face "eternal damnation." In spite of the composer's contumacious assertion of a lack of belief in "God the Judge," the Requiem quotation is associated with further, terrifying references to the Last Judgement in the last three symphonies – and with Tchaikovsky's representation of himself as "crucified Christ" (see p. 50). The trumpet cry at the beginning of the Fourth Symphony evokes the "Last Trump" on the Day of Judgement, when all carnal sins, *including homosexuality*, will be punished.[25] Similarly, in the Finale of the Fifth Symphony (mm. 219–30), the trumpet and horn calls echo the summons to judgement on the Last Day, while the written-out string tremolos "shiver" to the accompanying *terremoto*.

In the first movement of the *Pathétique*, punishment for the "sin" of homosexual incest becomes eternal damnation: the lovers' pastoral idyll is rudely interrupted by the double-forte half-diminished seventh chord initiating the development section, unleashing a vision of their torment in Hell.[26] The bass (mm. 160–70) unfolds the chromatic descending tetrachord D–C–B–B♭–A – a traditional Baroque *topos* signifying lament, death, and the Underworld. The fugue, with its coiling counter-subject, demonically recomposes Bob's playful ascending fifth sequence in the "scherzando" first group: D (m. 26 = m. 171) – A (m. 26 = m. 175) – E (m. 27 = m. 179) – B (m. 36 = m. 183) – F♯ (m. 42 = m. 185). Tchai-kovsky also draws upon other musical *topoi* to conjure up eschatological visions of Hell and the Last Judgement. The aggressive, descending trumpet lines in mm. 190–97 may represent "Fate" (as Brown asserts), but – since the Requiem citation follows immediately thereafter (mm. 202–05) – they also seem to allude to the events described in the Requiem, and especially to the "Last Trump." The "sigh"-motives (the "sospiri" A♭–G, C♭–B♭, D–C♯, etc.) introduced in mm. 217ff. express the anguish so emphatically documented by Tchaikovsky's contemporane-ous letters to Bob.[27]

Amorous combat: the march, militarism, and homosexual non-conformism

David Brown detects a "bizarre contrast" between the March for the 98th Yurevsky infantry regiment, which Tchaikovsky composed on the same day as he finished sketching the *Pathétique*, and the Sixth Sym-phony.[28] But no such "contrast" exists: the Yurevsky March (composed for the composer's cousin Andrey Petrovich Tchaikovsky, the com-mander of the regiment) and the March in the *Pathétique* are related in terms of genre and ethos. Furthermore, I shall propose that the *Pathé-tique*'s military and homo-erotic discourses are interconnected through the battle imagery of "amorous combat." With the March, Tchaikovsky draws upon a long tradition of battle pieces reaching back to the Renais-sance and continuing through Beethoven's *Wellingtons Sieg* and the *Alla marcia* in the Ninth Symphony, and his own *1812 Overture*, *Slavonic March*, and *Nutcracker Ballet* (the battle with the mice). Within the battle *topos*, the March signifies the "advance" or "charge" while, more unusually, the *Adagio lamentoso* evokes the fallen heroes (an inference drawn by the Third Reich, to be discussed in Chapter 6). The narratives of militarism, war, and tragic homosexual love intertwine as the March suggests homosexual non-conformism and defiant "crime" – *épater les bourgeois* as Klaus Theleweit has suggested – and the *Adagio lamentoso* "punishment."[29]

Let us consider the March in the larger context of Tchaikovsky's imperialism and militarism. In his cultural history of St. Petersburg, Volkov calls attention to Tchaikovsky's militaristic and "imperial inclinations" and Pan-Slavic aspirations as manifested in the early symphonies, observing that "Tchaikovsky's integration of those [folk] themes into the framework of his symphonies, Petersburgian in form and content, signifies his support for the unification of various nations under the aegis of the Russian tsar."[30] He calls attention to Tchaikovsky's quotation of the Russian anthem "God Save the Tsar" in the *Slavonic March* (1876) and *1812 Overture* (1880), which exploit the anthem's "emotional and symbolic possibilities" with its "psychological and political overtones." But Tchaikovsky's expression of Russian imperialism and Pan-Slavic chauvinism also permeates his later music, especially the *Nutcracker* (1892), the *Pathétique*, and the Yurevsky March (1893).

Tchaikovsky was devoted to Tsar Alexander III and sympathetic to his Pan-Slavic political program; as an indication of affinity with his monarch, he accepted and fulfilled various state commissions associated with Alexander's coronation in 1883. There was considerable mutual esteem between Alexander and Tchaikovsky and, as a sign of this, in 1888, the Tsar granted Tchaikovsky a lifetime pension of three thousand rubles a year (effectively replacing von Meck as Tchaikovsky's patron). Alexander surrounded himself with a coterie of Pan-Slavic advisers; an ardent anti-Semite, Alexander's assumption of power was marked by a rise in anti-Semitism and by pogroms throughout Russia on an unprecedented scale. In the 1880s, the "May Laws," intended to pauperize and dispossess the Jews, were passed; in 1887, new restrictions were enacted barring Jews from higher education and the professions.

Recognizing that Tchaikovsky's sympathies lay with Alexander's ideology is fundamental to interpreting the later music; indeed, Tchaikovsky's political and ideological affinity to Alexander's Pan-Slavism and his corollary anti-Semitism sheds considerable light on the subtexts of his later music. It is noteworthy that the *Nutcracker* remains impenetrable to those listeners who consider the work *per se* simply as an "innocent" children's ballet. David Brown expresses the perplexity of most naïve listeners when he asks, "Why on earth a young girl should, for a mild act of sentimental unselfishness and the heroic deed of hurling her shoe at the back of an unsuspecting mouse, be rewarded by the grossest offering of glitter and candy beggars comprehension. And since the piece leads to no true culmination, what was it all about anyway?"[31] However, the *raison d'être* for both scenario and music is revealed when one considers the ballet in the context of the ideology propagated by Alexander III and his circle. The Nutcracker – the Prince – is a thinly disguised stand-in for the Tsar, whose task it is to exterminate the mice, signifiers for the Jews. This equation of Jews with mice or rats, who in their greed, threaten to devour all of the gingerbread, i.e. the wealth of the country, is a long-standing Russian and central European phobia.[32] As George L. Mosse observes in his study of European racism, "the Jews were [like criminals] similarly degenerate characters; if they did not originate in the sewers of Paris, they were nevertheless compared to rats."[33] (Ignatiev, Alexander's Minister of the Interior, had insisted that the pogroms of the 1880s were the natural consequence of Jewish "greed," and he appointed commissions to investigate Jewish "exploitation" of Russians as the cause of the pogroms – rather than the pogroms' perpetrators.) This interpretation further explains Tchaikovsky's pairing of the *Nutcracker* with *Iolanta*, the motivation for which otherwise remains obscure: both (companion) pieces are concerned with "curing" a "disease." In *Iolanta*, the aim is to "cure" the homosexual "disease" of the individual body; analogously, in the *Nutcracker* the central goal is to "heal" the racial-economic disease of the body-politic by rooting out the parasitical vermin (the Jews) so that that the Prince or Tsar, as "father" of his people, can enjoy and share the "fruits" of his realm with his "children" or true subjects.

The goose-step march was not an invention of the Nazis; rather, it has a long history reaching back to the eighteenth century, if not earlier. The mechanistic, goose-step style of marching favored by Prussian drill-masters in the nineteenth century was also used by the Russian Imperial army, which had its own variants (and a variant of the goose-step was later taken over by the Red Army). Additionally, the stallions in cavalry units were trained to "march" in a version of the goose-step for horses (the choreography of the Spanish Riding School in Vienna being a famous offshoot of this tradition). The imperial symbolism of stylized, mass "swagger" of both men and stallions in an increasingly exaggerated display – which calls attention to the attributes of dominance, virility, and male bonding – is played out in the *Pathétique* on a grand scale through the progressive intensification of the March melody, which finally bursts forth in jaunty, unfettered glory.

Now in order to understand Tchaikovsky's integration of the military – i.e. battle – *topos* into the *Pathétique*'s over-arching erotic discourse, it is illuminating to consider the roles of the March and the *Adagio lamentoso* in the context of a long musical tradition of "amorous combat" reaching back, if not to the turbulent relationship of Mars and Venus, to the early Baroque. In his Eighth Book of Madrigals (*Madrigali guerrieri, et amorosi*) Monteverdi combines amorous and warlike narratives in a way that is not far removed from Tchaikovsky. Framing the battles of Tancred and Clorinda, marked by warlike episodes in the *stile concitato*, are quasi-amorous dialogue and lament in the *stile molle e temperato*. Within the *topos* of combat, the imagery of battle becomes a metaphor for "forbidden" sexual passion between Christian and Infidel – and especially for defloration ("Three times the knight squeezes the woman / in his mighty arms and each time / she frees herself from those binding knots . . ."). Clorinda is finally penetrated by Tancred's "sword" ("He thrusts his blade into her beautiful bosom; / it plunges in and greedily drinks the blood, / and the garment, beautifully embroidered with gold, / that confined her tender, light breasts / is filled with a warm flood"). In the *Pathétique*'s March and battle imagery, Tchaikovsky's homo-erotic narrative concerning Bob and his militant Pan-Slavism fuse in a triumphant "amorous combat" of the protagonists as victorious latter-day Achilles and Patroclus. But the symphony, like Monteverdi's *Combattimento*, concludes with a lament: in the *Adagio lamentoso*, Tchaikovsky's lovers are buried to the funereal sounds of the brass chorale; in the Monteverdi, the dying Clorinda, accompanied by the mourning "plaint" of four viols, expires begging for absolution.

It should be recalled, when considering the significance of battle imagery in the *Pathétique*'s homo-erotic discourse, that homosexual love has been a way of insuring fanatical loyalty between soldiers. Benedict

Friedländer, for example, in his influential book *Die Renaissance des Eros Uranos* (1911), went so far as to argue that homosexuality is essential to all military organizations. The Spartans institutionalized homosexual relations between men and boys to "bond" military units, an idea that has covertly if not overtly permeated many subsequent military and para-military societies and organizations.[34] For example, the storm-troopers (SA), who put Hitler in power, were led by the homosexual ex-soldier Ernst Röhm and his coterie of homosexual ex-army buddies, a violent politically reactionary group associated with the most heinous militarism and fascist chauvinistic violence (like some of their forebears in the officer corps of the Prussian and Russian Imperial armies).

In employing in the *Pathétique*'s March his own version of the "patter-rhythm" textures of the *stile concitato*, Tchaikovsky is following in the footsteps of other eighteenth- and nineteenth-century composers of battle music, most notably Beethoven in *Wellingtons Sieg*. Other striking features of Beethoven's martial language reappear in Tchaikovsky. For example, the extended harmonically unstable passages employing voice-exchanges between the bass and upper voices over a chromatically descending bass in the "Battle" episode of *Wellingtons Sieg* (mm. 74ff.) resurface at the climactic conclusion of the *Pathétique*'s March (mm. 304ff.). A further Beethovenian aspect of the Tchaikovsky is the idea of using ascending sequences to represent the "charge to victory." The large-scale harmonic structure of the Beethoven is controlled by a sequence of ascending fifths leading from C at the entrance of the French forces (mm. 31ff.) to G just prior to the "Charge" (mm. 192ff.) to D in the "Victory Symphony" (mm. 363ff.). Within this over-arching ascending fifth sequence, Beethoven delineates the "impulse" of the "Charge" itself by means of a sequence of ascending major thirds leading from the G of mm. 192ff. through B (mm. 228ff.) to D♯/E♭ (mm. 232ff.). The "impulse" of the "Charge" is further represented by the rising semitone sequence which fills in the first leg of the major third sequence (G–B), whereby the "Charge" melody is sequenced up by semitone beginning on A♭ (mm. 200ff.). In the *Pathétique*'s March, Tchaikovsky analogously represents "charge to victory" through the overall tonal ascent from E at the beginning of the March to G at its climactic conclusion. Here again, the "thrust" of the "Charge" is realized through a rising sequence – in this case of ascending fourths

(E–A–D–G) leading from E to G, which, as observed in Chapter 3, are motivically related to the March theme itself.

Within Tchaikovsky's amorous discourse concerning his relationship with Bob, the March's "Charge" to victory is loaded with homosexual overtones. In the visual arts, as we may observe in the battle frescoes of such homosexual or bisexual artists as Michelangelo, Leonardo, and Vasari, battle scenes provided an opportunity to celebrate masculinity and homo–eroticism through large groups of male nudes. Furthermore, in the visual arts – as in music (e.g. Monteverdi's madrigals of "Love and War") – the distinction between the martial and erotic in the interaction of these male nudes can be blurred. The design of Michelangelo's *The Battle of Cascina*, for example, supports this statement. Here Michelangelo depicts a large group of Florentine warriors bathing, caught by surprise by the attacking Pisans. Of particular interest is the blurring of the idyll – with its connotations of homosexual amour – and the battle in one and the same design. A similar overlap of martial and erotic *topoi* characterizes the Tchaikovsky March, which celebrates not only military but homo–erotic prowess.

In the March, the composer's homosexual love for Bob and his militant Pan-Slavic chauvinism are celebrated in a lovers' "parade." This signification of the March as a symbol of militaristic, anti-bourgeois, proto-fascist male-bonding was certainly not new in the German tradition, perhaps the most famous earlier example being the March from Beethoven's Ninth Symphony, "Froh, froh, wie seine Sonnen fliegen." But totally novel is the violent "revocation," the anti-Ninth gesture of the *Adagio lamentoso*, which overturns "the inferno-galop" (Thomas Mann's description); that the swashbuckling March should be left unpunished is unthinkable for Tchaikovsky, and the protagonists are "crucified" in the *Adagio lamentoso*.

Ecce homo!: the crucified artist

"What we have here is an abiding, inexhaustibly accentuated lament of the most painfully *Ecce-homo* kind" – with this observation, Mann links "revocation" with the Passion of Christ. The idea that the artist could "crucify" himself in his work reaches back to the Renaissance; it is intimated by Dürer's self-portrayal as Christ.[35] In the *Pathétique*,

Tchaikovsky draws upon this iconographic tradition, making the "Cross"-motive emblematic of himself and his beloved as crucified "*Men* of Sorrows" – and as *unredeemed* homosexuals; thus, homosexual passion is associated with the Passion of Christ.[36] To represent the idea that crucifixion becomes the only possible outcome to the "decadent" uncle–nephew love-affair, Tchaikovsky imports the "Cross"-*topos* from the sacred music of the Baroque and deploys it in conjunction with tonal imagery appropriate to a ballet, a fatal *pas de deux*. To better understand these crucifixion and *pas de deux* narrative strands, let us consider the cruciform characterization of the protagonists. Tchaikovsky's motive is the Tristanesque "yearning" ascending third followed by a descending second introduced in mm. 1–2, which I designate motive "T" ("Tchaikovsky-Tristan").[37] Notice that "T" contains embedded within it the Baroque *topos* of the "Cross"- this motive articulated as E–G–F♯–A or, perhaps, more obviously, as G–F♯–A–G.[38] In the first movement of the Sixth Symphony, the "sospiri" or "sigh"-motives in mm. 207ff. combine to form interlocking chromatic statements of the Cross-motive: F–E–G–F♯ etc. (violins, violas, mm. 211ff.).

Tchaikovsky's use of cruciform symbolism in *Romeo and Juliet* has a direct bearing upon the Sixth Symphony: in both *Romeo and Juliet* and the *Pathétique*, cruciform motives evoke the image of "crossed" or "doomed" lovers. In *Romeo and Juliet*, the theme first presented in D♭ major (mm. 213ff.), often referred to as the "love theme," might be further interpreted as "Romeo's perception of Juliet," or, more simply, as the "love/Juliet-Zak" theme.[39] Considered in this light, the "love" theme has much in common with the Bob-music of the first movement's second group in the *Pathétique*: both are highly lyrical, idyllic portraits of beloved, angelic youths. A particularly fascinating aspect of "Juliet's" melody is the cruciform aspect of the arpeggiation embedded in the theme's primary phrase (flutes: $a\flat^3$–c^3–$e\flat^3$–$a\flat^2$), which recurs in varied guises throughout.[40] These cross shapes in the love theme take their cue from Shakespeare's prologue, and specifically its characterization of the lovers as condemned by Destiny and "star-*cross'd*":

> A pair of star-cross'd lovers take their life . . .
> The fearful passage of their death-mark'd love
> And the continuance of their parents' rage,

> Which, but their childrens' end, nought could remove,
> Is now the two hours' traffic of our stage.

This "star-crossed" imagery is then further developed and transformed in Juliet's great soliloquy (Act 3, Scene 2, 1–25) where it becomes a triumphant, "starry" vision of sexual ecstasy and extinction:

> Give me my Romeo; and when I shall die
> Take him and cut him out in little stars,
> And he will make the face of heaven so fine
> That all the world will be in love with night,
> And pay no worship to the garish sun.

The Cross-motive is also essential to Tchaikovsky's 1870 revision of the musical characterization of Friar Laurence.[41] The appearance of the Cross-motive in the new introduction casts a dark shadow over the rest of the overture, suggesting that, as the instrument of Divine Judgement, Friar Laurence presides over, perhaps even instigates, the sacrificial "crucifixion" of the lovers.[42] This emphatically sinister view of Laurence and his role as instrument of divine "justice" is supported by the terrifying effect of his reiterated chorale-like theme in the revised development.[43] The second version of the development dispenses entirely with the "love/Juliet" theme to focus instead on the contrapuntal combination of the "fight" motive (and related material) with Friar Laurence's new theme (from the new introduction). Indeed, Friar Laurence's theme now acts as a *cantus firmus*: no fewer than nine sternly reiterated statements, primarily in the brass (horns and trumpets) but also in the winds and strings, penetrate the texture.[44] The implication that Romeo and Juliet have been "crucified," i.e. eternally damned, by the Friar-as-Angel-of-Death for their "sin" of "forbidden" (i.e. "homosexual") love lurks closely beneath the surface of the 1880 revision of the conclusion; of particular interest is the emphasis placed on the "broken" cruciform cells embedded within the jagged collapsing octaves of mm. 475ff.

The Cross-motive is taken up in the development section of the first movement of the *Pathétique*, which depicts the lovers condemned to infernal regions. Here, the close proximity of this evocation of the Cross (in the emphatic "sospiri" or "sigh"-motives of mm. 207ff.) to the Requiem citation (mm. 202–05) intimates that the lovers have been crucified for their "sin." In the second movement, the waltz melody extends Tchaikovsky's "yearning" third motive "T" (B–C♯–D–C♯) to a rising sixth (F♯–D–C♯) and then projects a diatonic version of the "Cross"-motive (D–C♯–F♯–E). Observe the additional cross shape (C♯–D–B–C♯) within the initial melodic segment. The exuberant lovers' *pas de deux*, first presented in the scherzando section of the first movement, continues in a more mellow vein in the second; here, each protagonist gracefully "dances" to the same eight-measure phrase of the melody before the music is allowed to proceed on to the next phrase. The interrelated ideas of high-spirited *pas de deux* and tongue-in-cheek transformation of the Cross-motive are continued at the beginning of the March: the initial figuration in the violins (mm. 1ff.) contains a diminution of B–A–C–B. Tchaikovsky's use of orchestral antiphony and paired thematic statements again evokes the *pas de deux*, creating the impression of a lovers' "chase." The "chase" continues through the initial presentation of the March theme *in toto* (mm. 71ff.), where it is first stated jauntily by the winds and then by the strings. Notice that it is only when the structural dominant D has been achieved – i.e. at this late juncture in the "chase" – that the strings finally "catch up" to the winds to erupt in the triumphant orchestral *tutti* statement of the March melody (mm. 229ff.).[45]

The lovers' *pas de deux* continues through the Finale. The "cruciform" shapes in the string parts at the Finale's beginning reactivate the "star-crossed" connotation of the "Juliet" theme (ex. 4.1b, p. 54): Tchaikovsky's highly unusual way of dividing the lines between pairs of parts not only describes the lovers as interlocked in their "crucifixion" but also represents the very essence of their love as "star-*crossed*." In the violin parts, the "Cross" is represented in two dimensions. Firstly, the individual parts articulate "cruciform" patterns, for example, the first violins express the "cross" e^2–$g\sharp^1$–$c\sharp^2$–$e\sharp^1$, a pattern stated by all four voices. Secondly, the voices themselves "cross" so that the first and second violins intertwine to create linear progressions. The Cross-motive is also present, with an enlarged medial interval, in the flutes and bassoons (mm. 4–12, ex. 4.1f). The lovers are depicted, superimposed both *in flagrante* and *in extremis*: coupled and crucified they are mirrored in the overlaid "pairs" of freely inverted Cross-motives (mm. 1–4, ex. 4.1b). This mirror imaging continues through the sequential music beginning with Bob's "angelic" D major (mm. 5 and 24), the free inver-

Ex. 4.1: *Tristan*-isms in the *Pathétique*

(a) *Tristan*, Prelude, mm. 1–13

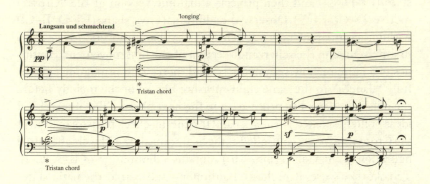

(b) *Pathétique, Adagio lamentoso*, mm. 1–2

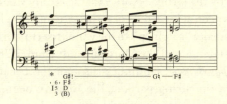

(c) *Pathétique, Adagio lamentoso*, mm. 50–54

(d) Op. 73 No. 4, "The Sun has Set," mm. 1–4

(e) *Tristan*, Prelude, mm. 36–40

(f) *Pathétique, Adagio lamentoso*, mm. 4–9

sion of the Tristanesque "glance" motive in the outer voices (see below), intimating the lovers' reciprocal tenderness even as they writhe in death-agony.

The beginning of the B section (mm. 37ff.) unravels the A section's motivic superimposition in a gentle *dux–comes* lovers' dialogue (*cf.* ex. 5.3, p. 79). The Cross-motive is initially chromatically inflected (F♯–F–E–G–F♯: 'celli and basses, mm. 40–42) and then imitated in pure diatonic form (F♯–E–G–F♯ etc.: violins and violas, mm. 42–44). As

Tristanesque chromatic "longing" motives are introduced (mm. 67ff.), the dialogue becomes increasingly impassioned; the *pas de deux* then breaks off with angry, despairing diminutions of Bob's descending-octave motive (mm. 77ff.). In the restatement of the "dysfunctional" seventh-chord music (mm. 104ff.), Tchaikovsky eliminates the Cross-motive in the individual voices, but the "Cross" reappears in a new guise in the large-scale "crossing" linear progressions contained within the climactic prolongation of the Neapolitan (mm. 115–25): as the conceptual upper voice (upper strings) plunges linearly from c^4 (m. 115, first violins) to g^2 (m. 124), another large-scale linear progression (brass and winds) ascends from E (m. 115, trombones) to g^2 (m. 124, flutes), the vertices of this massive cross intersecting on F in m. 118.

"Diseased" *Tristan*-deformations

In the *Pathétique*'s Tristanesque *Eros*-narrative, the passion "suffered" by Tchaikovsky's lovers (like Wagner's) is an incurable "disease" that slowly "poisons" them to become the agent of their destruction. In *Iolanta* – Tchaikovsky's most overt *operatic* trope on *Tristan* – a "cure" still seems possible; but in the *Pathétique*'s *symphonic Tristan*-deformation, the "disease" proves terminal. As observed in Chapter 1, the "moral and physical sickness" of homosexuality was stereotyped by physicians in the later nineteenth century and extended to many other realms of discourse including music.[46] This terrifying "medical" narrative strand embodies Tchaikovsky's critical response not only to the music of *Tristan*, but to its Schopenhauerian ideological framework – especially Schopenhauer's "theory" of *redemptive* longing and suffering – which underpins the later Wagner operas. While working on the *Pathétique*, Tchaikovsky also conceived a second *Tristan*-deformation: his setting of the Rathaus poems (which eventually became the Six Romances Op. 73). This song-cycle also projects the separated lovers tormented by Tristanesque anguish, their ecstatic meeting and momentary night of bliss, and their final separation and condemnation to eternal perdition. The intertextual dialogue between *Tristan*, the *Pathétique*, and Tchaikovsky's other *Tristan*-deformations mutually illuminates their semantic contents.

The "*Tristan*-chord" in the *Pathétique*

Perhaps the most distinctive and famous feature of the *Tristan* score is the so-called "*Tristan* chord" F–B–D♯–G♯, which, re-spelled as a half-diminished seventh chord F–C♭–E♭–A♭, appears at the climax of the Prelude (ex. 4.1a, p. 54). The chord's dissonant, plangent quality epitomizes the lovers' predicament: their adulterous, forbidden love, condemned by all social mores, is nevertheless so overpowering and compelling that they cannot escape from it; they can only surrender to its demands in full realization that this capitulation must result in their mutual destruction. But even in passionate embrace, the lovers are unable to achieve total satisfaction; in death alone are they destined to find release – and transfiguration. Throughout *Tristan*, the "*Tristan* chord" reappears at crucial points, usually at its original transpositional level.

In the *Pathétique*, and specifically its *Adagio lamentoso*, one is immediately struck by the fact that the initial chord is the same anguished "*Tristan*" sonority, i.e. the half-diminished seventh chord, transposed up a minor third: D–G♯–B–F♯ (ex. 4.1a-b).[47] In its new context, this sonority is essentially a "dysfunctional" seventh chord because its seventh, F♯, is neither properly prepared nor directly resolved; rather, this chord can be understood as a B minor tonic chord "with an added sixth" (G♯) in first inversion. Tchaikovsky's "dysfunctional" seventh chord becomes a metaphor for the "incurable dysfunctionality" of his protagonists' homosexual passion; hence, I shall refer to it as the "*Pathétique*" chord. Furthermore, as in *Tristan*, the emphatic reiterations of the chord bespeak the lovers' anguish at their inability to escape from the closed circle of their destiny. Like Wagner, Tchaikovsky calls attention to the "*Tristan* = *Pathétique*" chord with no fewer than ten unforgiving statements (mm. 1, 3, 20, 22, 104, 106, 127, 129, 131, and 133). In *Tristan*, Wagner focuses attention on the chord's original transposition, returning to it at crucial points in the drama; similarly, in the Finale of the *Pathétique*, Tchaikovsky latches onto the original transposition: of these ten iterations only the last two involve transposition down a fifth.

The "glance" and "yearning" motives in the *Pathétique*

Other strikingly Tristanesque features appear in the outer movements of the *Pathétique*. Ex. 4.1e shows the escape-tone version of the "glance" motive in mm. 36ff. of the *Tristan* Prelude; notice the use of rising sequence. Ex. 4.1f traces a similar characteristically Tristanesque rising sequential treatment of the "glance" motive in mm. 5ff. of the *Adagio lamentoso*. In *Tristan*, the ascending third filled in chromatically, and the so-called "longing" motive (m. 2), represent the lovers "yearning" to be together (ex. 4.1a); in the *Adagio lamentoso*, the "longing" motive reappears at the climax of the middle section (mm. 50ff., ex. 4.1c). In a more generic way, the Sixth Symphony's opening echoes the beginning of *Tristan* (ex. 4.1a): in *Tristan*, the ascending third "longing" motive participates in a "yearning" ascending third sequence; similarly, at the outset of the *Pathétique*, the ascending third "longing" motive is presented three times within a "yearning" rising sequence filling in an ascending third. This stepwise ascending third followed by a descending second (which I designated motive "T") functions, of course, as a fundamental motive in the symphony as a whole.

The "yearning" auxiliary progression in *Tristan*, *Manfred*, the *Pathétique*, and the Op. 73 song-cycle

Tristan and the *Pathétique* are controlled by the same "yearning" auxiliary cadence $\hat{3}$–$\hat{5}$–$\hat{1}$. Notwithstanding its massive length of over six thousand measures divided into three acts, *Tristan* is unified by the large–scale auxiliary bass progression $\hat{3}$–$\hat{5}$–$\hat{1}$: diatonically, E–G–C and, chromatically, E–G♭ = F♯–C♭ = B. As a macro-symphonic super-sonata form comprising over one thousand measures, the *Pathétique* is analogously structured by the auxiliary cadence $\hat{3}$–$\hat{5}$–$\hat{1}$, D–F♯–B (Appendix A). This structural parallelism (in conjunction with other more surface connections identified above) suggests that Tchaikovsky has incorporated the very essence of *Tristan* – Wagner's auxiliary cadential symbolism for Schopenhauerian "yearning" – into the harmonic fabric of his last symphony.

In tonal music, the tonic represents the ultimate point of departure and repose. The tonic is the reference point from which the music usually begins and to which it must return in the end. All harmonic digressions and adventures are measured against and derive their meaning from their relationship to the tonic. Sometimes, for expressive purposes, the music begins "off-tonic" and, by means of an auxiliary cadence, works its way back to the tonic at the end. The *Tristan* Prelude can be understood as an auxiliary cadence in C: III$\sharp^3$ (m. 1) – IV (m. 94) –V (m. 104).[48] The expected tonic, C, is withheld until m. 167 in the first scene; at this point Wagner takes steps to destabilize it to prevent a premature sense of repose. The absence of the C major tonic at the beginning of this auxiliary progression creates an impression of instability, restlessness, and longing for stability. The ceaseless, varied repetition of this cadential model represents unfulfilled "yearning."

The opera as a whole moves from C to B/C♭. Act 1 after the Prelude is essentially mono-tonal, rooted in C major-minor. Act 2 moves to C (m. 587), progresses towards B (enharmonically C♭, m. 1631), but is deflected deceptively to D minor. Like Act 2, Act 3 moves to C (m. 1285) and this time definitively cadences in B/C♭ at the end of the *Liebestod* (m. 1681). Notice that the III–V–I cadential model is recomposed at least nine times in Act 1.[49] This kind of deep structural III–V–I, which extends over the second and third acts as well, might be regarded as a form of ritualized keening over the lovers' fates. Act 2 begins with a massive recomposition of the cadential model as ♭III (m.1) – III (m. 555) – V (m. 585) – I (m. 587). The triumphant arrival on the tonic (m. 587) coincides with Tristan and Isolde's first passionate embrace at the beginning of Scene 2. In m. 998, the music regains E (III), but instead of moving on to G (V) it progresses to A♭ at the "Nachtgesang" (m. 1122). Initially, this A♭ functions as if it were G♯ or upper third of the preceding E major; however, in m. 1371 in the first presentation of the *Liebestod* music, it is reinterpreted as VI moving to V in B (mm. 1472–73). At the moment when the lovers are discovered *in flagrante* (m. 1631), the B is displaced.[50] At the catastrophic revelation, the anticipated B is deflected to F, which then becomes the first term of the model auxiliary progression III (m. 1631) –V (1688) – I (m. 1689) transposed to D minor, which initiates the final scene. Act 3 opens with a massive recomposition of the cadential model: IV (F, m. 1) moves down (as upper neighbor) to III (E, m. 914), which then progresses to V (G, m. 1006) and thence to I (C, m. 1285).[51] Significantly, the arrival on the tonic coincides with Isolde's long-delayed entrance and the beginning of the lovers' final embrace. The return to E in m. 1305 initiates a second colossal statement of the model progression, chromatically deformed as in Act 2: E (m. 1305) – G (m. 1619) – A♭ = G♯ (m. 1621) – G♭ = F♯ (m. 1663) – C♭ = B (m. 1681).

Ex. 4.2: Auxiliary cadences in *Manfred* and the Six Romances, Op. 73

(a) *Manfred*, first movement

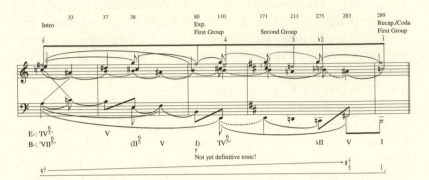

(b) Six Romances, Op. 73

As in *Tristan*, in *Manfred* the large-scale auxiliary cadence becomes a tonal metaphor for the protagonist's "restlessness" – his anxious "yearning." Ex. 4.2a displays the large-scale harmonic plan of *Manfred*'s opening movement. According to this interpretation of the harmony, the definitive arrival on the B minor tonic is delayed until the very end of the movement (m. 289). The initial sonority proves to be a IV "$^6_5$" or "chord of the added sixth" in the key of E minor rather than a seventh chord. The emphatic B minor chord in m. 80 is not yet the definitive tonic arrival; rather the auxiliary cadence continues in m. 90 as the music moves to another subdominant "chord of the added sixth" now built on E, which functions as IV "$^6_5$" of the final tonic B minor. The large-scale harmonic progression, then, is a massive auxiliary cadence A–E–F♯–B (E minor: IV$^6_5$–B minor: IV$^6_5$–V–I) into the B minor tonic.

In the *Pathétique* and the Op. 73 song-cycle, Tchaikovsky re-activates the *Tristan-topos* of the "yearning" large-scale III–V–I auxiliary cadence: the large-scale harmonic plans of the first and last movements of the *Pathétique*, "We Sat Together" (Op. 73, No. 1), and the song–cycle as a whole are identical (compare ex. 4.2b with Appendix A). Song 1 begins in E major, moves to G♯ (m. 24) as dominant (m. 25), and cadences on C♯ (i.e. C♯ minor: III–V–I). As described in Chapter 3, the bass in the outer movements of the *Pathétique* moves from D major to F♯ to B (i.e. B minor: III–V–I). The Op. 73 song–cycle as a whole also composes out a III–V–I auxiliary cadence in A minor: ♯III (C♯, Song 1) – V (E, Song 4) – I (A, Song 6, ex. 4.2b).

Large-scale harmonic organization and narrative: the structural dominant and the lovers' tryst

In *Tristan*, the *Pathétique* and the Op. 73 song–cycle, the arrival on the structural dominant within the large-scale auxiliary cadence has a panto-mimic significance, representing the crucial instances in the erotic drama when the lovers are reunited.[52] In *Tristan*, the decisive moves to the structural dominant and tonic in Acts 2 and 3 coincide with the lovers' physical embraces. In Act 2, the entire first scene constitutes an extended prolongation of E♭ moving up to E (C: ♭III–III); the harmony then "waits" expectantly – as Isolde impatiently awaits Tristan – to move up to G (V), the V and I being "released" just at the point when the lovers are triumphantly reunited (mm. 585–87). In Act 3, the initial 840–measure prolongation of F minor (C: IV) "yearns" to rise to G (V) but is prevented by the long delay in Isolde's arrival. The music regains E (III, m. 914) and is permitted to reach G (V, m. 1006) – recomposing the Prelude's auxiliary III–V progression – only once Isolde's sail is finally sighted. The tonic C, the resolution of the V, is then achieved after a massive – over 200-measure – dominant prolongation, just prior to Isolde's appearance on stage (m. 1285). (Isolde is, of course, "too late," which is why her entrance *follows* the definitive bass move to C.) But here as in Act 2, the fundamental idea is the coordination of the structural V–I cadence with the lovers' embrace.

In the *Pathétique* and the Op. 73 song–cycle, as in *Tristan*, the defini-tive moves to the structural dominant within the large-scale auxiliary progressions analogously indicate those points in the narrative when the lovers – who have been painfully separated – are finally reunited.[53] In the first movement of the *Pathétique*, a series of "fateful" fanfares (mm. 274–76) introduces the crucial passage (mm. 277–304) on the structural dominant (Appendix A, a). Here, Simon Karlinsky makes the valuable point that *this* is the instance in the narrative when the protagonists embrace.[54] Drawing on the *topoi* of Mozart's *Don Giovanni* (especially the trombones as harbingers of death) and Beethoven's Fifth Symphony, the fanfares – more specifically, the triplet reiterated diminished chords in mm. 270 and 274–76 (in oboes, horns, and strings) – signify a fateful "knocking," which arouses the Oracle, which then delivers the dire pronouncement (in the trombones, mm. 280ff.). It prophesies and decrees an agonized "love-death" to be fulfilled in the coda to the *Adagio lamentoso*. As in Act 2 of *Tristan* (mm. 587–89), when the protagonists consummate their love, their union becomes both fateful and ultimately fatal; and, as in *Tristan*, having drunk from the cup of love, the lovers have knowingly quaffed a "poison" that will become the agent of their destruction: the die is cast, and the music is fraught with the symbolism of the death-pronouncing Oracle.[55]

In the Op. 73 song-cycle, the affirmation of the structural dominant (in Song 4) within the "yearning" auxiliary cadence (E as V/A) analogously coincides with the lovers' tryst (ex. 4.2b): "Filled with the sweet bliss of this blessed night, / you have rested your head on my shoulder. / I am supremely happy, dearest love, / eternally happy with you this night." As if to underscore the structural-dramatic parallelism with *Tristan* at this triumphant juncture, the piano part (m. 1, etc.) clearly parodies the opening of the *Tristan* Prelude: in a near-literal quotation, the right hand ascends chromatically G♯–A–A♯–B over E major harmony (compare exx. 4.1a with 4.1d).

The metaphysics of register : the Wagnerian registral "embrace" of the damned

There can be no doubt that for Wagner, Tchaikovsky, and many later nineteenth- and early twentieth-century composers, register had profound symbolic and metaphysical connotations. Employing Schopenhauerian terminology, we may conceive the phenomenal world as basic reality. The phenomenal – the "basis" of mundane perception – may be associated with the musical "bass." Since the noumenal is intuited by

cale harmonic structure of the first movement of the Fourth Symphony
s organized over a "deformed" plagal or perfect cadence, i.e. a tritonal
rogression, which may be understood either "plagally" as I–♯IV–I or
perfectly" as I–♭V–I, depending on the interpretation of the enhar-
nonically equivalent ♯IV (B) or ♭V (C♭, Appendix B, a). A similar tritonality governs the "love" scene between Carmen and Don José in
Carmen's Act 2. As McClary observes, in the famous so-called "Flower
Song" monologue, D♭ major supports Don José's narrative of how the
flower (which Carmen had thrown him in Act 1) consoled him in prison
("La fleur que tu m'avais jetée") within a larger G context.[61] In other
words, the tonal structure of the scene is designed to project G–D♭ tritonality on a large scale, or – metaphorically – to "entrap" Don José's D♭
within Carmen's G. In the Fourth Symphony's first movement, the bass
partitions the octave F–F symmetrically into two conjunct tritones, F–B
and B–F, and then subdivides these into sequentially ascending minor
thirds: F (first group, mm. 28–115) – A♭ – C♭/B (second group and
development, mm. 116–294) – D (recapitulation of second group, mm.
295–312) – F (coda/recapitulation of first group, mm. 365–end).
Tchaikovsky's symmetrical bass partition also seems related to Bizet's in
Act IV of Carmen: here, the bass, centered on F, symmetrically partitions
the ascending minor ninth F–G♭/F♯ into two disjunct ascending tritones
F–B and C–G♭, each of which is symmetrically bisected into two ascending minor thirds F–A♭–B and C–E♭–G♭/F♯.[62]

Carmen speaks to Tchaikovsky not simply as an opera about "Fate"; in
Bizet's tritonal representation of Carmen's "freakish" racial identity
and her concomitant animal sensuality, Tchaikovsky senses an inspiring
parallel to his own coded depictions of his own fateful "anomaly." In
Swan Lake, homosexual tritonality is reincarnated in Odette's Carmen-
esque animal sexuality (i.e. in her "birdlike" passion) and her anomalous nature (semantically marked by her racial indeterminism as
"white–black" swan). Her B–F tritonality is worked into the ballet's
structure on a grand scale so as to invoke a terrifying racial and sexual
subtext: Odette, the "white" swan, and Odile, the "black" swan, are
revealed to be two sides of the same racially-sexually schizophrenic bird-
woman.[63] In the light of day, the putatively "white" Odette is exposed in
the guise of her "black" alter-ego Odile, i.e. as a demonic monster, who
seduces the prince, ultimately destroying him and herself. In the Pathé-

rising above the mundane, i.e. is perceived from great spiritual "height,"
it is associated with the extreme high register. If basic reality – the phenomenal – corresponds to the lowest register, and transcendental reality
– the noumenal – is associated with the highest register, then the
emphatic *ascent* (the musical-rhetorical figure of *anabasis*) in the *Tristan
Liebestod* from the very lowest to the very highest registral bands may
represent the arduous path from the everyday world to the higher plane
of the visionary, i.e. from the illusion of the phenomenal to the ultimate
reality of the noumenal. In the *Pathétique*'s critical deformation of
Tristan, the converse, i.e. the striking *descent* (*catabasis*) from the highest
to the lowest register, signifies numbing collapse.

The later nineteenth century was fascinated by the idea that, in the
sexual embrace, the lovers' identities merge within a greater unity in
which their individualities are erased. In Munch's *The Kiss* (1898), for
example, the identities of the lovers are blurred. Schopenhauer's influence lurks behind Munch's own description of the picture: "both of
these [lovers] are depicted in the instance when they are not themselves,
but only one of thousands of bodies in the chain which binds the
sexes."[56] A similar blurring of identities is depicted in Klimt's "Diesen
Kuss der ganzen Welt" from the *Beethoven Frieze* (1902). Extending this
visual symbolism to music, Wagner in *Tristan*'s *Liebestod* and Tchaikovsky in the *Pathétique* represent the "embrace" of their lovers by analogously *blurring* registral distinctions between the structural upper voice
and the bass.

Let us first consider the concluding music of Act 3 of *Tristan*, which,
in turn compresses the end of Act 2, Scene 2. As the noumenal is
achieved by Tristan and Isolde in their sexual embrace (end of Act II,
Scene 2) and final death-kiss (end of Act 3), the tones of the descending
$\hat{5}$-line in the upper voice are registrally shifted upward into the very
highest registral band: f♯[1] (m. 1632) – e[2] (m. 1663) – c♯[4]–b[3] (m. 1681).
Prior to the upper voice achieving the extreme high (noumenal) register,
however, the tones of the fundamental line E–D–C♯ ($\hat{4}$–$\hat{3}$–$\hat{2}$) are shifted
into the bass (mm. 1664–68). Redemption of the phenomenal (the bass)
by its experience of the noumenal (upper voice) is composed into the
very fabric of the musical structure in a registral "reaching under,"
whereby the tonal functions of the fundamental line are momentarily
transferred from the very highest to the very lowest voice. Since this

unorthodox registral shift – this "coming-together" of the structural voices – corresponds to an "embrace" in registral terms, I designate it the "registral embrace"-metaphor.

Analogous registral symbolism informs the *Pathétique*. Here, the registral embrace-metaphor, which represents the "blurring" of the lovers' identities as they are united, is realized through a series of collapses into the lowest register, these registral plunges extending over the course of the symphony. Notice the striking descent in the introduction: the structural upper voice assigned to the violas' D–C♯ ($\hat{3}$–$\hat{2}$, m. 13) immediately drops two octaves to "embrace" the bass. The structural upper voice again "embraces" the bass in the second group's love music, the high f♯³ (m. 130) languorously cascading down four octaves to F♯ (bassoons, m. 160). This idea is then recomposed with great intensity over the structural dominant (mm. 284–304); as the lovers are sexually united, the structural upper voice again "embraces" the bass register: f♯³ (violin 1, m. 284) – f♯¹ (m. 296) – e¹ (m. 297) – D (bassoons, 'celli, m. 299) – C♯ (m. 301, $\hat{4}$–$\hat{3}$–$\hat{2}$). This tonal imagery of the upper voice descending to "embrace" the bass carries through the reprise of the second group to the coda, where it gives rise to the descending octave figure in the pizzicato strings (mm. 335ff.).

The Finale posits the last, fatal meeting of the separated lovers. As in the third act of *Tristan*, the long-delayed encounter occurs over the move to the structural dominant (mm. 115ff.) and the lovers enjoy their final embrace in death. But for eternally "damned" Tchaikovsky and Bob, there is no transfiguration – just collapse (see also Song 6 of the Six Romances, to be discussed shortly): they expire as the first violins plunge from the high c⁴ ($♭\hat{2}$, m. 115) to the trombones' low C (m. 139). This registral collapse, foreshadowed by the previously discussed descents in the first movement, continues *ad infernum* into the coda, until the low strings fade into oblivion (*niente pppp*).

The unsuccessful attempt to "cure" homosexual tritonality

In the Fourth Symphony's first movement, the move to B major in a movement in F minor attaches sinister connotations to the representation of the idyllic "dream boy": F–B tritonality becomes emblematic for Tchaikovsky's Fate-decreed homosexual "sickness"; Symphonies

Nos. 4 and 5 attempt a "cure" but the malady ultimately pr[...] s the *Pathétique*.[57] Within the meta-symphonic narrative span[...] phonies Nos. 4–6, the "thread of Fate" (*Fatum*) is the tonal de[...] of large-scale sequences.[58] Within this sequential Destiny-me[...] tonal "breaks," "interruptions," or "overlaps" in the sequence[...] the homosexual "illness" "tricking" or "double-crossing" the[...] nist, while the attempt to "correct" the tritonal links with perfe[...] or fifths constitutes a sustained but ultimately unsuccessful[...] "cure" the "disease."

Tritonality as a harmonic "abnormality" representing hor[...] "deviance from a norm" becomes emblematic for Tchaikovsky's[...] sexual problem" in all its complexity. Bearing in mind the time-[...] musical convention of the tritone as "the devil in music" (the[...] *in musica*), it is entirely appropriate that the composer should ha[...] ciated homosexual and racial problems with "deviant" tritonal ha[...] progressions. The narrative strand of homosexual tritonality, i[...] relatively early in Tchaikovsky's career, first appears in the overtu[...] ballets, only later being transferred to the symphonies. It is alr[...] *topos* in the overture to *Romeo and Juliet* (1869, revised 1870 and[...] and the ballet *Swan Lake* (1875–76) before it conditions the sust[...] attempt at a "cure" in the last three symphonies (1877–93). In *Rom[...] Juliet* and *Swan Lake*, tritonality symbolizes the protagonists' "b[...] iled" love. The intensification of *Romeo and Juliet*'s tritonality thr[...] the 1870 and 1880 revisions resonates with the tritonal representa[...] of "forbidden" love in *Swan Lake*, the later symphonies and their s[...] lite orchestral works, e.g. in the Fifth Symphony and the *Hamlet O[...] ture* (composed in 1888, the same year as the Fifth Symphony), and[...] interrelated *Voyevoda* Symphonic Ballad (1891) and the *Pathét[...] (1893). In *Hamlet*, for example, Tchaikovsky recomposes the large-s[...] F–B "homosexual tritonality" of the Fourth Symphony's first m[...] ment to represent the "misogynist" (i.e. "homosexual") comp[...] (Hamlet-Tchaikovsky) rejecting his wife (Ophelia–Antonina).[59]

Tchaikovsky's *engagement* with Bizet's *Carmen* perhaps as earl[...] March 1875 – certainly by January 1876 – resonates in his own music[...] the last three symphonies, Tchaikovsky restages *Carmen*'s "fateful"[...] tonally symmetrical bass progressions (which relate to Carmen's ani[...] allure and racial "Otherness" culminating in her murder).[60] The lar[...]

tique as *Eros*-symphony, the irresistible tritonal attraction pulling Don José to Carmen becomes the tritonal force binding Tchaikovsky to Bob Davidov . . . and the outcome follows *Carmen* rather than *Tristan*, death being *not* redemptive but nihilistic: in the final bars of *Carmen*, Don José murders Carmen as a form of suicide (i.e. he kills her *en plein air* in full knowledge of the capital punishment he must inevitably incur); in the intense tritonality of the *Adagio lamentoso*, there is no transfiguration, just unredeemed oblivion.

The nineteenth-century conception of homosexuality and gambling as "diseases" informs Tchaikovsky's last operas and symphonies. In *The Queen of Spades* and the last three symphonies, sequences of perfect fourths and fifths are assaulted by "homosexual" or "gambling" tritonality. In *The Queen of Spades*, for example, an ascending-fifth sequence "cures" and "redeems" Hermann's "gambling" tritonality, which threatens him with eternal damnation. The first two acts constitute a larger tonal unity, which moves through an ascending fifth from B (beginning of Act 1) to F♯ (end of Act 2). The third act continues the prolongation of F♯, which then ascends another perfect fifth to conclude on C♯/D♭ (thus, harmonic Destiny is determined by the ascending fifth sequence B–F♯–C♯/D♭). Within this framework, the tritone F♯–C attempts to overwhelm the last leg of the sequence (i.e. the perfect fifth F♯–C♯).[64] In light of his eleventh-hour conversion, Hermann is forgiven; the bass "corrects" C to C♯/D♭, "healing" the diminished F♯–C with the perfect fifth F♯–C♯/D♭: by renouncing gambling through apology and by reaffirming his love for Lisa, Hermann "cures" and "redeems" his tritonality, transmuting it within the perfection of the ascending fifth sequence.

The conception of homosexuality as "blindness" – a medical condition requiring a cure – informs *Iolanta's* plot. The heroine, congenitally "blind," has never "seen": having been hermetically sealed from birth in her secluded garden-oasis (like a "bubble child"), she is totally unaware of her "blindness." As the Moorish doctor Ibn Hakia explains to her father, King René, she can be "cured" of her "affliction" only if she is able to recognize it as an ailment. Then she is saved not by science but by the grace of God and the love of a man. Related to this notion, within the meta-symphonic sequential Destiny-metaphor spanning the Fourth through Sixth Symphonies, the harmony tries to "cure" "sick" tritonality through "healing" sequences of perfect fifths and fourths.

The Fourth Symphony's slow movement "heals" the first movement's "sick" F–B tritonality by expanding the diminished fifth B–F to the perfect fifth B♭–F in its ternary form (Appendix B, b): B♭ (A section, mm. 1–125) – F (B section, mm. 126–98) – B♭ (A′ section, mm. 199–end). But, by sequentially partitioning the octave F–F symmetrically into ascending major thirds (Appendix B, c), the Scherzo's sequence "undoes" the slow movement's "perfect" (B♭–F) "cure": F (A section, mm. 1–132) – A – C♯/D♭ (B section, mm.133–217) – F (A′ section, mm. 218–end). In the rondo-Finale, F–B♭ plagality finally succeeds in "curing" the first movement's F–B tritonality by composing out the perfect fourth B♭–F, which "overcomes" the tritone B♭–E (Appendix B, a and d).[65] If "sick" E–A♯ tritonality dominates the Fifth Symphony's sonata-form outer movements (Appendix C, a and d), it is ultimately "healed" by E–A plagal perfection in three dimensions: (1) the tonal motion from the third movement's A major to the Finale's E major (Appendix C, c-d), (2) the A–E–A tonal structure of the Waltz's ternary form (Appendix C, c), and (3) the emphatic plagality of the Finale's coda-to-the-coda (mm. 546–end, Appendix C, d). This "healing" plagality is also worked into the slow movement's B minor/D major bitonal background (Appendix C, b), the "pain" of B–F/E♯ tritonality in mm. 1–55 and mm. 1–152 being transferred to D-G♯ tritonality in mm. 8–91 and mm. 8–158 and finally "healed" by over-arching D-G plagality in mm. 8–99 and mm. 8–164.[66]

In the *Pathétique*, the homosexual-incestuous "anomaly" of the lovers' relationship "provokes" Destiny, which responds to the "provocation" by re-enacting the Fifth Symphony's E–A♯ tritonality in the *Pathétique*'s introduction, and by superimposing a large-scale pronouncement of B–(E♯)/F tritonality (of the Fourth Symphony's first movement and the Fifth Symphony's slow movement) upon the *Pathétique*'s "healthy," i.e. "normative" perfect fifth B–F♯ (I–V, assuming B in the bass in the first movement's m. 19, Appendix A, a). The March defiantly attempts to "cure" tritonality by continuing the large-scale sequential Destiny-metaphor of descending "perfect" fifths initiated from B (of the first movement) –E–A–D–G (G major: (III)–VI–II–V–I, Appendix A, a and c). But the protagonists' palliative – even arrogant – affirmation of their "happily perfect" Destiny is violently confuted by the intense tritonality of the *Pathétique* = *Tristan* chord at the beginning of the Finale: Fate intervenes in the sequential "Destiny-metaphor," the March's sequence of perfect fifths being prevented from continuing through the *Adagio lamentoso*. In the *Pathétique*'s tragic Finale, the "anomaly" proves to be "incurable:" the outer voices seize upon C–F♯ as the last, tritonally "deformed" leg of the March's sequence of descending fifths (i.e. (E–A–D–G–) *C–F♯*, B minor: ♭II–V), inscribing its fatal, tritonal "perversion" of the perfect fifth upon the lovers' death certificate as "cause of death."[67]

In *Iolanta*, as in *Tristan*, the "cure" depends not on the perception of physical "light" but the inward, Schopenhauerian "light" of the noumenal. The doctor discloses that Iolanta must be able to "see" this light with her soul:

> Two worlds, that of the flesh and that of the spirit, have been united in all manifestations of life by a superior will, just like two inseparable friends. There is no sense that the body alone knows, nor is the gift of sight limited to the body. And before opening mortal eyes to light, this sense should be understood by the eternal soul. When the intelligence has become aware of this truth, only then . . . can the will open the shadows of the body to light.[68]

Released from her betrothal to Robert, Duke of Burgundy, Iolanta's metamorphosis into a "seeing" being coincides with her transformation into a socially acceptable companion for her lover Vaudémont; the implication is nothing less than a re-polarization of her sexuality from ingenuous homosexual (i.e. from "unconsious blindness") to conscious heterosexual: capable at last of bonding with her male lover, she is "cured" and able to "see." In *Iolanta*'s re-formation of the *Tristan* plot, a "forbidden" relationship is transformed (by Robert's renunciation of his claim to Iolanta) into a socially acceptable one. In *Tristan*, the lovers, although condemned on earth, experience transfiguration in the realm of death; in *Iolanta* they are analogously "healed" through faith. But through critical deformation of *Tristan* in the *Pathétique* and the Six Romances, the homosexual condition proves "incurable": there can be no transfiguration; rather, the lovers are condemned to the eternal "darkness" of their "illness" and the nihilistic oblivion of death.

If the fourth song of the Six Romances presents the lovers' physical encounter, the fifth song, "Amid Sombre Days," depicts a meeting in the realm of dreams. In this dream-state, the "absent beloved" becomes

Ex. 4.3: Enharmonic transformation and spiritual 'illumination' in Op. 73, No. 5, "Amid Sombre Days," mm. 31–34

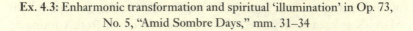

I passionately desire to live again, to breathe through you

such an integral part of the protagonist's own being that his ability to "breathe" through the beloved's incarnation in his own being reawakens a passionate desire to live. In this fashion, he can go on living, albeit alone:

> In the charm of bright dreams,
> It seems as if I am together with you,
> In the light of day and in the quiet of night,
> I am again with you [in spirit],
> My sadness fades away into the dark distance;
> I passionately desire to live again,
> To breathe through you, and to love.

Tchaikovsky incorporates the protagonist's potentially redemptive "transfiguration" (through his incorporation of the beloved) – specifically, his ability to "perceive" the light of the noumenal – into the essence of the musical structure through the technique of enharmonic transformation (ex. 4.3): in mm. 32–33 of the A♭ major setting, the vocal line is elevated to a high $b\flat\flat^2$ ($\flat\hat{2}$), which is then enharmonically "illuminated" as a^2 ($\sharp\hat{1}$), ascending triumphantly to $b\flat^2$ (in the piano's right hand) in m. 34.[69] Reconstruing $B\flat\flat$ as an ascending passing tone A forces the listener to revalue the "dark," Neapolitan $B\flat\flat$ major ($\flat$II) as "bright" A major, i.e. as the "raised" tonic ($\sharp$I). The "raised" tonic optimistically represents the protagonist's ability to "see": his spiritual "illumination" and possibly his sexual re-polarization.

But in Song 6, this Tristanesque "illumination" (i.e. this ability to "see") dissipates in "darkness"; Song 6 tragically undercuts Song 5 just as (in the *Pathétique*) the *Adagio lamentoso* incapacitates the March. Although the key of A concretizes the enharmonic "victory" of A over $B\flat\flat$ won in Song 5, the minor mode setting evokes unmitigated despair through its obsessive Josquinesque F–E ($\hat{6}$–$\hat{5}$) "miserere mei" motive, a climactic unresolved leading tone in the vocal line ($g\sharp^2$, m. 21), harmonic immobility (the A pedal throughout), and composed fade-out (*diminuendo al pp*, ex. 4.4, p. 72). If the allusion to the *Tristan* Prelude in Song 4 (ex. 4.1d) is exuberantly tongue-in-cheek – in their ecstasy, the light-hearted lovers had been able to mock the "heavy" Wagnerian legacy – retrospectively, in view of Song 6's "pathetic" consecration of final parting and threat of eternal damnation ("My dear, pray for me; / I am always praying for you"), *Tristan*-deformation is revalued as bitter critique: *Tristan*'s *Liebestod* lies; Iolanta will never "see" – there is no "cure."

The homosexual "sickness" narrative and the rejected E♭ Major Symphony

Those who have argued that Tchaikovsky lived his later years and died a "happy" homosexual have insufficiently considered the phenomenon of the cross-genre transformation of the "happy" E♭ Major Symphony. Arguably, the symphonic was the most important genre in the composer's output, followed immediately by opera, with the genres of the concerto, orchestral suite, ballet, and chamber music etc. playing an ancillary role. By this reasoning, the primary discourse in Tchaikovsky's life-work was the ultimately tragic narrative concerning the protagonist's inability to "cure" the homosexual "disease" unfolded in the meta-symphony spanning Symphonies Nos. 4–6. Although this tragic disquisition holds pride of place within the oeuvre, the less privileged

71

Ex. 4.4: "Miserere mei" motive and unresolved leading tone in Op. 73, No. 6, "Again, as before, alone"

(a) mm. 1–2

(b) mm. 21–24

Where are you now, my darling? I cannot begin to put into words everything that happens to me

genres, like the piano concerto or the orchestral suite, were of course free to present other, optimistic narratives; as already mentioned, the opera *Iolanta* argues that a "cure" is possible, and the concertos and orchestral suites are essentially "happy" works.

That Tchaikovsky did not really believe the music of the E♭ Major Symphony to be of irredeemably poor quality is demonstrated by his efforts to convert it into concert pieces for piano and orchestra. The satellite genre of the piano concerto could readily assimilate the "happy" music originally intended for the symphony. But the cross-genre metamorphosis of the E♭ major music from the symphonic into the piano concerto genre reveals Tchaikovsky ultimately refusing to assimilate its optimistic narrative into the primary, symphonic discourse: its music had to be "banished" from the symphonic genre since this was to be reserved for the tragic "autobiographical" narrative concerning the relationship with Bob. By "exiling" the cheerful music of the E♭ Symphony, Tchaikovsky made it clear that, within the privileged symphonic discourse, there could be no "cure" for the homosexual "disease"; rather, the E♭ major "Seventh" Symphony had to be emphatically rejected from the canon of numbered symphonies not simply because its music was intrinsically inferior or lacking in substance, but also because its "happiness" failed to represent Tchaikovsky as fundamentally "unhappy" homosexual.

5

Compositional genesis: the Six Romances Op. 73 and the Pathétique

A fascinating aspect of the compositional process as documented by the sketches is that the genesis of the *Pathetique*'s *Adagio lamentoso* might be connected with the first two songs of the Six Romances and the Waltz with the third song. This possible role of the Op. 73 song-cycle in the compositional genesis of the symphony will be revealed as we explore the evolution of the work in the sketchbook.[1] The *Particell* (or short score) and a few sketches for the Sixth Symphony are contained in a sketchbook from 1893 comprising seventy-two written pages. The first movement is drafted on pp. 1–19. A number of sketches for the March are found on pp. 20–21. After two blank pages, on p. 24, Tchaikovsky sketched the introduction to the first movement and also entered another sketch for the March; thus, as recognized in the literature, the introduction was added as an afterthought. Pp. 25–46 preserve the full draft of the March. Pp. 47–49 and pp. 53–54 represent a mystery: do the cancelled sixty measures they contain constitute an early draft of the first part of a different Finale, which Tchaikovsky later rejected, or do they represent the short score of an unfinished "Concert Piece for Cello and Orchestra"?[2] Around these unidentified sketches, on pp. 50–52 and pp. 54–61, the definitive Finale took shape. The last segment of the sketchbook devoted to the *Pathétique*, pp. 62–69, contains the draft of the symphony's second, Waltz movement.

An especially interesting facet of the *Particell* is the order in which Tchaikovsky entered the sections of the music. In this regard, the first movement and the Waltz are the least complicated. The first movement was entered on pp. 1–19 in one continuous draft beginning with m. 19 (of the final version) and continuing through to the end. The introduction (mm. 1–18) was sketched later on p. 24. The Waltz – in all probability the last to be composed but clearly labeled "II" at the beginning of the draft

74

– was also set down in a single draft. The Waltz's A section (mm. 1–56) is notated on pp. 62–65, and its B section (mm. 57–96) on pp. 66–68. Sketches for the Coda are found on the bottom of p. 65 and on pp. 68–69.

By contrast, the March – the second movement to be composed – was written down in a much more complicated way. On pp. 20, 21, and 24, Tchaikovsky entered various preliminary sketches. His first step, on p. 20 systems 4–14, was to fix and define the goal of the movement, namely the final triumphant statement of the March theme in the G major tonic (approximately mm. 229–39). On systems 16–20 on the same page, he sketched a later passage (mm. 318–24) in the apotheosis of the March theme. Interestingly, Tchaikovsky designated these sketches "episodes for the Scherzo," although in the final version the apotheosis of the March theme certainly functions not as an "episode" but as the movement's primary theme. Once the goal of the large-scale auxiliary cadence to G had been fixed, the next step was to define the E minor music foreshadowing the March theme at the beginning of the movement. On the top four systems of p. 21, Tchaikovsky entered a passage (mm. 61–64) that occurs in Part 1's A section, circled it, and noted that it was "to be added to the first presentation of the March." On systems 5–8, he superimposed the figuration in mm. 1–3 upon both the E minor transposition of the March theme, and the second "b" theme (mm. 37–39) within the binary A section (Tchaikovsky identified this "b" theme with the note "to prepare for the repetition," ex. 5.1). Although these preliminary studies test the contrapuntal superposition of the two themes plus the initial figuration, this particular combination is not exploited in the finished work. On systems 1–15 and 19–20 of p. 24, Tchaikovsky sketched the introduction around an earlier sketch for the music leading into the cadenza in the March on systems 14–17 (mm. 205–26). All of these sketches probably antedate the drafts on the following pages.

The first *Particell* draft of the March, labeled "Movement III" (pp. 25–30), presents the music of Part 1's A section up to the beginning of its B, i.e. up to the first full statement of the March theme in E major (mm. 1–80). The presentation of the March theme in the "wrong" key of E major is very hastily indicated along with its accompanying figuration before the sketch breaks off. In a note dated 11 February at the bottom of p. 30, Tchaikovsky indicated the future course of the music. Before drafting this statement in its entirety, Tchaikovsky decided to leap

Ex. 5.1: Contrapuntal superposition of themes in the third movement (March/Scherzo), *Pathétique* sketchbook, p. 21

forward in the movement and to complete the triumphant apotheosis of the March theme in the "right" key, namely the home tonic of G major, i.e. in *Part 2*'s B section (which he had already begun to sketch on p. 20). Thus, pp. 31–37 contain a full draft of Part 2's statement of the March theme in G major in m. 229 continuing to the end of the movement. The later part of the movement now having been successfully written down, Tchaikovsky could reach back to mm. 47ff. already sketched on p. 29 (i.e. to the b section within Part 1's A section), and on pp. 38–41 sketch the varied transposition of this material in Part 2's A section and Cadenza (mm. 187–228). Only once this varied transposition had been notated was Tchaikovsky prepared to sketch the first full presentation of the March theme (mm. 71–133) in the "wrong" key of E major on pp. 43–46 of the sketchbook.

After completing the draft for the March, Tchaikovsky seems to have reached a hiatus in composing the Sixth Symphony. As Paulina Vaidman has proposed, he may have embarked on a different but possibly related project, namely a "Concert Piece for Cello and Orchestra," which is drafted after the March on the sketchbook's pp. 47–49 and pp. 53–54.[3] However, it is noteworthy that this draft occurs precisely at the point in the sketchbook where, having laid out the symphony's initial two movements, Tchaikovsky must have been thinking about the remaining movements, and especially the Finale. Therefore, this draft (in the "correct" key of B minor) *could* conceivably represent an initial idea for the A section of the final movement of the symphony. After rejecting this "Concert Piece" or Finale (we shall leave the issue undecided), Tchaikovsky proceeded to sketch the Finale as we know it. But he did not begin with the opening A section (mm. 1–38) as one might expect; rather, the first part to be set down was the B section (mm. 38–103). Possibly the very first draft of this passage occurs at the very end of the sketchbook on p. 70 systems 13–14. In an unusual way of writing, Tchaikovsky began to notate the B section on the *right*-hand page of the sketchbook, beginning on page 51 (mm. 37–54), and then continued the draft on the *left*-hand side, that is, on page 50 (mm. 55–72), before continuing in the normal way on page 52 (mm. 71–103).

On the still-free systems 7–13 of page 54, at the end of the draft for the "Concert Piece" or Finale, Tchaikovsky studied the pick-up in m. 19 (the last measure on p. 52), namely the way of dividing "crossing" linear progressions between two leaping parts (ex. 5.2, p. 78). Once this idea had been realized, he could then exploit it in the draft of the A section (mm. 1–37) on p. 55. After the A section had been set down, Tchaikovsky entered the varied reprise of the A and B sections and the Coda (mm. 104–end) in one unbroken draft on pp. 57–61. The movement was now complete.

The sequence in which the sketches and drafts were set down and their location on the pages of the sketchbook are fascinating for a number of reasons. By adding the introduction to the first movement after it was drafted, it is clear that Tchaikovsky's decision to link the beginning of the *Pathétique* motivically with the Fifth Symphony through the key of E minor and E–A♯ tritonality (as explained above) was the result of careful deliberation and planning. Furthermore, if the E–A♯ tritone suggests that the "wound" – supposedly "healed" in the Fifth Symphony Finale's coda – has reopened, the proximity of the introduction sketches to the sketch for mm. 305–06 of the March reveals that the role of the March (like the coda to the Fifth), with its emphasis on the perfect fourth E–A, is to "cure" the "wound."

The sequence of drafts for the March accords with Tchaikovsky's underlying concept of the large-scale auxiliary cadence with G functioning as goal (Appendix A, c). In conformance with this plan, Tchaikovsky's initial step was to establish the arrival on G with a preliminary sketch on p. 20. Then, as soon as the music up to the beginning of Part 1's B section had been drafted, Tchaikovsky was anxious to draft the

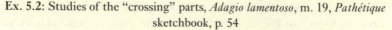

Ex. 5.2: Studies of the "crossing" parts, *Adagio lamentoso*, m. 19, *Pathétique* sketchbook, p. 54

goal of the large-scale auxiliary progression in its entirety, i.e. the full, triumphant presentation of the March theme in G (mm. 229ff.). For this reason, he leapt forward in the piece to complete the G major presentation of the March theme. Only once this harmonic and thematic goal had been "anchored" was he prepared to go back and fill in the details of the path to the goal.

The canceled draft for the "Concert Piece for Cello" or the Finale's A section eloquently suggests that Tchaikovsky had encountered a block in the composition of the symphony, necessitating a pause for reflection; the Muse had abandoned him, if only temporarily. I believe that the way forward was suggested by a programmatic connection between the Finale and the first of the Rathaus songs, "We Sat Together." In other words, I am proposing that the Six Romances provided models for the *Pathétique* just as Wagner's *Wesendonck-Lieder* did for *Tristan*.

The setting of the last stanza of the first Rathaus poem (mm. 17–end) is connected with the B section of the Finale (mm. 37ff., ex. 5.3). The dialogue of descending fourths (F♯–C♯) between the bass and inner voice of the right hand against the syncopated pulsating G♯ pedal point in the

Ex. 5.3: The B-section of the *Adagio lamentoso* is motivically related to the first song of the Six Romances, Op. 73

(a) *Pathétique, Adagio lamentoso*, mm. 39–42

(b) Op. 73, No. 1, "We Sat Together," mm. 17–22

And now I am once more alone, and expect nothing from the future. No longer is there any feeling in my heart

right hand (mm. 17ff.) closely corresponds to the B section of the *Adagio lamentoso* (mm. 37ff.). At the end of the song, the lovers sit together by a river wrapped in mute melancholy (the speaker reproaches himself bitterly for having said nothing at the time); the dialogue between bass and inner voice against the pedal articulates silent, inner communion (as it does in the related passage in the *Adagio lamentoso*):

> And now I am once more alone,
> And expect nothing from the future.
> No longer is there any feeling in my heart.
> Why, oh why did I then say nothing?

To represent the lovers' anguished longing – their Tristanesque *Sehnsucht* – Tchaikovsky activates the *Tristan-topos* of the "yearning" large-scale III–V–I auxiliary cadence in both the song and the *Adagio lamentoso*.

Tchaikovsky had begun to set "We Sat Together" in August 1892.[4] As he struggled to find the right music for the *Pathétique*'s tragic Finale, he was reminded of the song's last stanza. Having made this connection, he transposed the song's auxiliary cadence from C♯ minor to B minor (i.e. E major moving to C♯ minor becoming D major moving to B minor, compare Appendix A, d and ex. 4.2b); thus, he began the draft of the *Adagio lamentoso*, transposing the song-transformation from E major to D major (mm. 37ff.) on the sketchbook's pp. 72 and 50–51. At this point, the final version of the A section of the Finale had not yet been conceived. Only when he had reached the pick-up to the A section's return (m. 103) did Tchaikovsky conceive the idea of the "crossing" voices (sketched on p. 54, ex. 5.2). The *topos* of the Cross motive then inspired composition of the A section (mm. 1–36), which followed on pp. 55–56. The A section may be indebted to the second song, "Night": the descending right-hand figure, which plunges beneath the left hand's accompaniment, is clearly related to the descending motive in the *Adagio lamentoso* (bassoons, mm. 30ff., ex. 5.4). Close correspondence between this descending motive (associated with "descent" into death's eternal night in the Rathaus setting) and the descending motive in the *Adagio lamentoso* reinforces the interpretation of the *Pathétique*'s Finale as depicting the protagonists' demise.

Ex. 5.4: The A-section of the *Adagio lamentoso* is motivically related to the second song of the Six Romances, Op. 73

(a) *Pathétique, Adagio lamentoso,* mm. 30–36

(b) Op. 73, No. 2, "Night," mm. 1–5

Once the motivic-semantic connections between the first two songs of Op. 73 and the *Pathétique*'s *Adagio lamentoso* had facilitated a compositional break-through, both the Finale and the Waltz could be drafted quickly. The third song, "In This Moonlit Night," is clearly connected with the Waltz, the last movement of the *Pathétique* to be composed. Its exuberant rising sixth motives (E♭–C followed by G–E♭) – expressing the lovers' joy at their reunion – become the rising sixths (F♯–D followed by A–F♯) in the primary theme of the *Pathétique*'s Waltz (ex. 5.5). The semantic connection between the symphonic Waltz and Song 3 is unmistakable: just as, in the symphony, the Waltz evokes the amorous D major idyll (of the first movement's second group), in the song-cycle the third song celebrates the lovers' joyful meeting:

> In this moonlit night,
> In this wondrous night,
> In this moment of our meeting,
> O my dear, I cannot restrain
> My love, but must declare it.

Ex. 5.5: The waltz is motivically related to the third song of the Six Romances, Op. 73

(a) *Pathétique*, second movement (5/4 waltz), mm. 1–4

(b) Op. 73, No. 3, "In this Moonlit Night," mm. 1–2

At the end of the short-score of the *Pathétique*, Tchaikovsky expressed his gratitude to the Deity for granting him the inspiration to conclude the symphony: "Lord, I thank you! Today, on 24 March [1893], I completely finished the *Particell* [for the Sixth Symphony]."

Deconstructing *homosexual* grande passion pathétique

In view of the *Pathétique*'s enormous popularity with composers, conductors, orchestras, and the concert-going public, a complete review of reception and performance practice would extend well beyond the confines of the present study. Consequently, I shall restrict my remarks on the *Pathétique*'s "reception" to composers' creative reception, and to the interpretation – possibly "misinterpretation" (depending on one's point of view) – of this symphony by conductors and musical propagandists in the Third Reich.

Mahler's *Pathétique-pietà* and other twentieth-century resonances

Immediately after Tchaikovsky's sudden death under "mysterious" circumstances, the *Pathétique*'s "autobiographical" program was taken literally. Rumors of the composer's putative suicide proliferated; many inferred that the composer had killed himself because his homosexuality had become unbearable. Whether Tchaikovsky actually committed suicide is immaterial to the reception history of the *Pathétique*; since audiences believed it, the *Pathétique* evoked widespread sympathy as a foreshadowing explanation, i.e. as musical suicide note. That this tragic *Eros*-symphony depicted a homosexual *grande passion pathétique* culminating in suicide quickly captured the popular imagination; at the turn of the century, the *Pathétique* was in vogue, powerfully influencing Tchaikovsky's younger contemporaries and successors.

It is noteworthy that contemporary critical opinion quickly associated the *Pathétique* with tragic, "operatic" sources – even prior to Tchaikovsky's death. In his perceptive review of the premiere, Laroche immediately recognized that the *Pathétique* cloaks a tragic operatic narrative in a strictly instrumental guise, observing that it is precisely this dramatic pathos which motivates the symphony's novel formal structure and draws forth musical gestures extending beyond the purely symphonic idiom: "the form is somewhat mysterious . . . one is left with an impression of something alluring and uncommonly beautiful, *but which goes beyond symphonic boundaries* [my emphasis]."[1] Having referred to the symphony's "cross-genre" uncertainty, Laroche calls attention to the operatic element, describing the first movement's second group as "more operatic in style than symphonic." The tragic, operatic element is especially noticeable in the Finale, which, according to this critic, seems to accompany "something occurring on stage, such as, for instance, the slow death of the hero; here too . . . one senses not so much a symphonic as an operatic character."[2] In the spirit of *fin-de-siècle*, it became fashionable to imitate the *Pathétique*'s operatic "decadence." In the hands of Tchaikovsky's successors, Tchaikovsky's autobiographical homosexual passion for Bob is deconstructed back to its operatic interracial model. The homosexual Other now becomes the racial Other: the symphonic discourse depicts the "pathetic" passion of the Jew Mahler for the Gentile Alma and the Russian Rakhmaninov for the Gypsy Anna Aleksandrovna Lodizhenskaya. After Mahler, Rakhmaninov, and their generation, the *Pathétique*'s homosexual "*Tristan*-deformation" continued to resonate loudly in the twentieth-century repertoire, most notably in the music of Berg and Britten. The representation of autobiographical passion became an artistic necessity, a consciously manipulated *decadence*.[3]

In his perceptive study of Tchaikovsky's influence on Sibelius, Joseph Kraus aptly observes that "the tracing of musical influence is an inexact science at best, requiring proof of exposure to the earlier composition, and a reasonable demonstration that musical borrowing has actually taken place."[4] Kraus goes on to make a helpful distinction between superficial or coincidental similarities, which he calls "chance intersections," and musical borrowings involving transformation, which he describes as "profound integration." I would further propose that "profound integration" can take place on many different levels ranging from generic correspondence to semantic deconstruction and the re-use of particular musical techniques.

Sibelius: "chance intersection"?

Some scholars have alleged Tchaikovsky's strong influence on Sibelius, especially on the earlier music. John Warrack sums up the common wisdom when he observes that "with his Finnish birth, it is not surprising that this [First Symphony] should stand closer to the Russian than the German symphonic tradition."[5] Did the *Pathétique* influence Sibelius's First Symphony (1898–99)? Both are tragic works in which the symphonic protagonist is denied ultimate redemption; they are "anti-Ninths" – works of "revocation" – as described at the outset of this book. In a letter to his wife Aino written shortly after the premiere of his First Symphony outside Finland (in Stockholm on 4 July 1900), Sibelius complains that his own symphony has been criticized as being too obviously influenced by Tchaikovsky and suggests that the influence is fortuitous rather than real: "I know that there is much in that man that I also have. But there isn't much one can do about that. *Das muss man sich gefallen lassen.*"[6] In my view, the case remains open. Presumably Sibelius became familiar with the *Pathétique* at some point, but precisely when remains unknown. Jurgenson published the score in 1894 and it was first performed in Helsinki on 26 October 1894; but whether Sibelius was present at this concert or acquired the score at that time has not been ascertained. Unlike Mahler and Rakhmaninov, Sibelius was not personally acquainted with Tchaikovsky, and his knowledge of Tchaikovsky's music may have been quite superficial, especially in his early period.

Although Sibelius's early orchestral works might seem indebted to the Russians (especially to Rimsky-Korsakov but also to Tchaikovsky), his orientation was and remained decidedly Austro-German.[7] If certain semantic and technical features of the *Pathétique* can be discerned in Sibelius's First Symphony, these correspondences may well be Kraus's "chance intersections."[8] To be sure, one cannot discount the possibility that Tchaikovsky's formal innovations in earlier pieces such as *Manfred* provided models for the young Sibelius. Later, the syntheses of Scherzo and Finale in Sibelius's Third Symphony, and first movement and Scherzo in his Fifth, might seem indebted to Tchaikovsky's synthesis of Scherzo and first group in the *Pathétique*'s first movement. Furthermore, the large-scale auxiliary cadences spanning Sibelius's Fourth Symphony and the "triumph of entropy" in its Finale could be generically related, if not indebted, to the *Pathétique*'s *Adagio lamentoso*.[9] But I strongly suspect that Sibelius developed his formal and tonal innovations under the influence of composers active in the German tradition, especially Bruckner, Brahms, and Liszt, and that Tchaikovsky's influence on him throughout his career – contrary to received wisdom – was less strongly marked.

Rakhmaninov: the "Forbidden" passion of the two Annas

Rakhmaninov described himself as "not a student but a disciple" of Tchaikovsky.[10] It is clear that, in making autobiographical love-relationships the subject of symphonic music, Tchaikovsky and Rakhmaninov were thinking along similar lines in the early 1890s. In 1891 or 1892, Rakhmaninov was introduced to Anna Lodizhenskaya, the Gypsy wife of a friend, with whom he became infatuated. It is not known whether Anna welcomed the young composer's advances; however, a relationship lasting at least five years developed, which Anna broke off shortly after the failure of the First Symphony in 1897.[11] A considerable number of Rakhmaninov's most important early works are programmatically connected with his love for Anna, including the song "Oh stay, my love, forsake me not!" Op. 4, No. 1 (1891, revised 1892, and explicitly dedicated to Anna), *The Crag* Op. 7 (1893), and the First Symphony Op. 13 (1895), and the works reflecting gypsy influence, the opera *Aleko,* and the *Capriccio on Gypsy Themes* Op. 12 (1894).

After the performance of the two-piano arrangement of the *Pathétique* at Taneyev's house on 20 September 1893, Rakhmaninov also presented *The Crag*. Rakhmaninov recalled the occasion:

> I well remember my last meeting with P. I. Tchaikovsky, to whom I showed "The Crag" and who said, with his gentle smile: "What hasn't Seryozha written this summer! A poem and a concerto and a suite, and Heaven knows what else . . . And I wrote only one symphony.[12]

Ippolitov-Ivanov describes the calming influence Rakhmaninov's work had on Tchaikovsky that night:

> Because of the many halts to correct some detail or for the cavilings of Pyotr Ilyich, who for some reason was especially nervous that evening, the symphony made no impression on us, and Pyotr Ilyich was gloomier than a storm cloud.

That evening I made the acquaintance of Sergei Vasilyevich Rakhmaninov, who had graduated from the Moscow Conservatory a year before my
arrival in Moscow . . . At the close of the evening he acquainted us with the
newly completed symphonic poem, "The Crag" . . . The poem pleased all
very much, especially Pyotr Ilyich, who was enthusiastic over its colorful-
ness. The performance of "The Crag" and our discussion of it must have
diverted Pyotr Ilyich, for his former good-hearted mood came back to
him.[13]

Tchaikovsky may have been impressed by *The Crag* because its depiction of tragic love was close in spirit to the pathos expressed in his own
new symphony.[14] He made arrangements to perform *The Crag* in St.
Petersburg in January and promised to conduct it on his forthcoming
European tour.[15]

There are many points of contact, both in terms of program and technique, between Rakhmaninov's First Symphony and Tchaikovsky's
Pathétique and – on the largest scale – between the meta-symphonic narrative which unfolds in Rachmaninov's three symphonies culminating
in the Symphonic Dances and Tchaikovsky's last three symphonies. Following the example of Tchaikovsky's last symphonic trilogy, the Rakhmaninov symphonies and Symphonic Dances are unified in terms of
both narrative and tonality.[16] In Rakhmaninov's symphonic oeuvre, it
seems appropriate to posit "profound" (even "critical") "integration" of
Tchaikovsky rather than "chance intersection." Just as Marx claimed
to stand Hegel "on his head," Rakhmaninov critically "inverts"
Tchaikovsky's meta-symphonic discourse; while the protagonists collapse at the end of the *Pathétique* and Rakhmaninov's First Symphony,
the remaining Rakhmaninov symphonies and the Dances play out a
redemption metaphor of "healing" and "resurrection." In other words,
if the meta-symphonic narrative in the last three Tchaikovsky symphonies documents the course of a fatal "disease" culminating in the protagonists' demise, the three Rakhmaninov symphonies and Symphonic
Dances deliberately reverse this process. Precipitated by the failure of
his First Symphony and rejection by the woman he had hoped would be
his mistress in 1897, Rakhmaninov suffered from chronic depression
and experienced a creative block from roughly 1897 to 1900.[17] But it
would not be an exaggeration to say that much of his music composed
after 1900 celebrates his "healing" and "resurrection" from a variety of
perspectives.[18]

Rakhmaninov's First Symphony is closely connected with the *Pathé-tique*. Composed in the shadow of the *Pathétique*, its narrative embodies a catastrophic violation of the *ad astra* paradigm: in both symphonies, the slow coda to the Finale intimates the death if not the possible suicide of the beloved. Just as Tchaikovsky encodes his putatively fatal homosexual passion in the *Pathétique*, Rakhmaninov's First Symphony takes as its subject its composer's "decadent" and ultimately doomed ardor for the racial Other, in this case for the Gypsy Anna Lodizhenskaya, her racial stigma being clearly marked by the music's "orientalisms" (especially noticeable in the "feminine" second group material in the symphony's sonata forms). And just as Tchaikovsky dedicates the *Pathétique* to Bob, Rakhmaninov inscribes his First Symphony to his beloved yet married "friend" "A. L." (Anna Lodizhenskaya). By accompanying this dedication with an inscription taken from Tolstoy's *Anna Karenina* (a quote from the Song of Moses in Deuteronomy, "Vengeance is mine, I will repay"), Rakhmaninov associates the two Annas: Anna Lodizhenskaya with the heroine of Tolstoy's novel, suggesting that, as in the novel, the adulterous liaison will have fatal consequences.[19] While, in the *Pathétique*, Tchaikovsky projects the homosexual lovers' punishment and demise (in the *Adagio lamentoso*), Rakhmaninov depicts his own and/or his beloved Gypsy's collapse (suicide?) in the catastrophic *Largo* coda of his Finale.[20]

Rakhmaninov's programmatic deconstruction of Tchaikovsky's homosexual pathos back to its interracial operatic model continues in the Second Symphony (1907) by racially stigmatizing the "forbidden" Beloved. The macro-symphonic narrative then concerns the "consecration" of this "forbidden" yet ultimately "healing" love relationship.[21] In the Second Symphony, the "forbidden" is stigmatized by a motivic reference to Rakhmaninov's anti-Semitic opera *The Miserly Knight* (1900–05); specifically, the symphony's primary theme assumes the turn motive, which in the opera, had characterized the "evil" Jewish money-lender Salomon. This motivic borrowing is strikingly exact: the opening of the symphony is clearly derived almost note-for-note from the passage in the opera where Salomon suggests to Albert that he poison his miserly father to gain his inheritance:

> THE JEW: Lord, you like to joke with me.
> No, no, I wanted . . . I only thought, perhaps
> That it was time for the Baron to die.[22]

The "sinister" Salomon-motive prevails at the end of the first and second movements (first movement, Rehearsal 23 + 14 and second movement, Rehearsal 44 + 12). But "forbidden" love – now stigmatized by the Jewish (rather than the Gypsy) reference – is triumphantly "converted" and "assimilated" through the remainder of the symphony.[23] This process of "converting" the "forbidden" yet beloved Other continues and is reaffirmed in the Finale, where the "healing" assimilation of the Salomon-motive is triumphantly celebrated through its transformation into a chorale (Rehearsal 89 + 4).

Continuing the meta-symphonic narrative, the Third Symphony applies the "healing" metaphor to the *Pathétique*'s militaristic battle imagery. As Barrie Martyn observes, the second movement contains a March, which is "the Rakhmaninov equivalent of the third movement of Tchaikovsky's *Pathétique* Symphony, a virile march of enormous energy and impetus."[24] Interestingly in terms of form, the Rakhmaninov conflates the second Adagio movement and the third March movement. Whereas Tchaikovsky's triumphant March is tragically undercut by the *Adagio lamentoso*, Rakhmaninov's March is gently enfolded within the lyrical *Adagio non troppo*: wounds "heal" and swords are beaten into plowshares. The narrative circle is closed as the first of the Symphonic Dances transforms the fatefully "wounded" opening of the First Symphony into a *cantabile* "healed" coda to the first Dance (Rehearsal 27).

Rakhmaninov's symphonies "profoundly integrate" many other aspects of the *Pathétique*'s formal and tonal language and semantic allusions. A few of these may be mentioned here. Rakhmaninov's use of fugato in the development of the First Symphony's first movement and Third Symphony's Finale and in the Second Symphony's Scherzo is clearly indebted to the fugal exposition in the development of the *Pathétique*'s first movement. Additionally, the representation of Hell in the development section of the Second Symphony's first movement (Rehearsal 17ff.) is also derived from the corresponding section in the *Pathétique*, as well as *Francesca da Rimini*. The first movement of the *Pathétique* may have influenced the first movement of Rakhmaninov's Second Symphony from a formal-tonal perspective. Chapter 3's analysis of the *Pathétique*'s first movement showed how the sonata form "passed through" the first group's recapitulation, delaying the definitive tonic arrival until the second group's recapitulation. Similarly, in the initial movement of Rakhmaninov's Second, the recapitulation of the first theme is abridged to occur above the dominant pedal (Rehearsal 17 + 16) at the end of the development section; as in the *Pathétique*, tonal stability is achieved only with the second group's recapitulation in the tonic major (Rehearsal 20 + 10).

Mahler's *Pathétiques*

In his Sixth through Tenth Symphonies, Mahler – like Rakhmaninov – deconstructs Tchaikovsky's homosexual *passion pathétique* back to its interracial model, the meta-symphonic discourse running through his Fifth[25] through Tenth Symphonies (1901–11) being propelled, in part, by the tension between himself as Jew and Alma as Gentile.

Mahler conducted important performances of Tchaikovsky's symphonies, operas, and concertos, including the *Pathétique*. For example, he created the first German productions of *Eugene Onegin* and *Iolanta* in Hamburg in 1892 in Tchaikovsky's presence. Tchaikovsky was profoundly impressed with Mahler, describing him as a man "of genius with a burning desire to conduct the first performance [of *Eugene Onegin*]."[26] Given his interest in Tchaikovsky, Mahler probably became familiar with the *Pathétique* immediately after its publication (by Jurgenson in 1894). That he had studied the symphony by 1901, if not earlier, is revealed by the contemptuous reference to it in a conversation recorded by Natalie Bauer-Lechner: Mahler complained that it was "a shallow and extroverted, terribly homophonic work."[27] To Guido Adler, who had praised the *Pathétique*'s orchestration, Mahler condemned its orchestration as failing to compensate for deficiencies in content:

> That's just humbug (*Geflunker*), sand in the eyes. When you take a closer look, very little remains. Those arpeggios through all the heights and depths, those meaningless sequences of chords can't disguise the emptiness and lack of inspiration. If you take a colored dot and swing it round an axis, it looks like a shimmering circle. But when it comes to rest it's just the same old dot again, and even the cat won't play with it.[28]

But, in spite of this harsh critique, Mahler clearly admired Tchaikovsky's symphonic music sufficiently to want to conduct it in Vienna that year. In January 1901, Mahler had conducted *Manfred*; he intended to conduct the *Pathétique* in March and was only prevented from doing so by illness (in the event, it was Franz Schalk who led the performance). Regarding Mahler's apparent about-face, La Grange observes that "at the beginning of his career, Mahler rarely showed such antipathy towards a work, but [with respect to the later performances], it must be borne in mind that he almost never conducted a piece that was not to his taste, at least not after his Hamburg period."[29] This change of opinion is confirmed by the six performances he conducted during his last two New York seasons (1910–11); at the same time, Mahler lovingly introduced *The Queen of Spades* to his American audience (it was to be his last opera production), despite some critics carping about his "Slavic sympathies." In a review of the second performance of the *Pathétique* (7 March 1910, the day after the premiere of *The Queen of Spades*), the *New York Times* critic observed that "[Mahler] has previously been instrumental in producing the works of the greatest Russian composer at Vienna, and it is probable that he feels strongly in sympathy with them."[30]

A strong case can be made for the *Pathétique*'s direct influence on Mahler. In a review of a 1910 performance of the *Pathétique*, one of the New York reviewers, while missing an appropriately "Slavic melancholy" in Mahler's reading, nevertheless called attention to his "analytical" interpretation, remarking that this symphony "never had been dissected in such an analytical way."[31] Conducting the *Pathétique* enabled Mahler to "internalize" and "profoundly integrate" its various aspects into his own musical language. But Mahler's compositional reception of the *Pathétique* extends beyond mere appropriation of the adagio-Finale in his Third, Sixth, Ninth, and Tenth Symphonies; if the concluding funereal chorale of the Finale of the Mahler Sixth closely approximates the *Adagio lamentoso*'s ethos of total abnegation as it dispels the euphoria of the first movement's coda and the Andante, the Ninth and Tenth Symphonies not only "profoundly integrate" the *Pathétique*'s "failed" *ad astra* narrative – they "overcome" it (in a Nietzschean sense).

The meta-symphonic narrative in the later Mahler symphonies (like the last Tchaikovsky symphonies), deals with a "difficult" autobiographical issue: here, the "problem" is Mahler's sexually and racially problematic relationship with Alma: she, the tall, beautiful Gentile – the Mary-figure - he the neurotic, driven and busy, moneyed, con-

91

siderably older, shorter (and later sick), "thrice outcast" Wandering Jew. Mahler's autobiographical meta-symphonic narrative resonates with the deep-rooted European phobia of the Jew "seducing" and "defiling" the Gentile – with fatal consequences for the Jew (in the valedictory Tenth Symphony, as in the *Pathétique*, the composer portrays himself as "crucified") – a phobia reaching back at least to the eighteenth century, if not earlier. (The Nazi "theory" of racial "hygiene" culminating in the Nuremberg Laws clearly responded to this fear.) In the later symphonies, Mahler codes his thematic material autobiographically in terms of both gender and race, making the first group his own, the second Alma's (thus, for autobiographical reasons, he reverses Otto Weininger's characterization of the first theme as "Gentile" and the second as "Jewish").[32] In the Sixth Symphony, for example, he explicitly identifies the first movement's affirmative, exuberant second theme as a characterization of Alma, which is sharply contrasted with his own grim first group march material; Mahler himself describes the trombone solos in the Seventh as one of that symphony's "typically Jewish things. (I am a Jew you know)."[33] This reading of the meta-symphonic narrative receives strong support from Mahler's programmatic exclamations in the manuscripts of the Sixth through Tenth Symphonies (and from recently released biographical information). Noting the importance of these comments for interpretation, Peter Franklin condemns their suppression in the published scores as a symptom of "the cultural embarrassment that underlies the doctrine of non-referentiality in German symphonic music."[34]

The *Pathétique's* influence can be felt on Mahler's Sixth Symphony: like the *Pathétique*, Mahler's Sixth features harmonic parallelism between the outer movements and a "tragically" undermined recapitulation in the first movement. Recall again that the *Pathétique's* first movement tragically "passes through" the tonic at the beginning of the recapitulation (m. 245, see Chapter 3) and its outer movements are structured over the same "inexorably fateful" harmonic progression (I^6–V–I). Mahler's first movement analogously passes through the tonic at the recapitulation of the first group (prolonged in mm. 291–359) by reinterpreting it as the dominant of the subdominant (which supports the abridged reprise of the second group, mm. 360–78). The large-scale harmonic thrust in the exposition and development is I–(VI)–IV–V–I.

As in the *Pathétique*, the first movement's harmonic structure becomes "fatefully" paradigmatic for the Finale, which reproduces the first movement's harmonic progression.[35]

The *Pathétique*'s "failed" *ad astra* narrative is even more "profoundly integrated" in the Adagio-Finales of Mahler's Ninth and Tenth Symphonies. The Rondo-Burleske third movement of the Ninth embodies a diachronic transformation: in a conceptually "previous state" of the macro-symphonic form, the Rondo leads without break into the Adagio-Finale. In this "previous state," the third statement of the ritornello (the A3 in the outline presented below), represented by the third *fugato* (mm. 311–46), evolves into a transition to the break-through/Adagio-Finale (mm. 347ff.); tonally, A minor would function as the minor dominant leading to the definitive tonic arrival on D major in the putative Adagio-Finale, this D major realizing the *ad astra* narrative. In the movement's "endstate," however, the putative Adagio-Finale "fails" and gradually re-incorporates back into the still-unfolding Rondo: euphoric D major begins to unravel by about m. 429, decaying slowly but inexorably toward D minor. The "true," third ritornello (A3, mm. 522–616) then reinterprets D minor as the subdominant and reasserts the hegemony of A minor (the definitive arrival on the tonic being "saved" for the coda, mm. 617ff.).

The return to the Rondo-Burleske (mm. 522ff.) embodies Mahler's "profound integration" of the *Pathétique*'s "failed" *ad astra* narrative. In the *Pathétique*, the March is overthrown by the tragic Adagio-Finale. Analogously, in the "endstate" of the Rondo-Burleske, the putative Adagio-Finale is undercut by the reasserted Burleske as D major's potentially redemptive yet fragile reconstruction of the Fifth Symphony *Adagietto*'s ethos collapses. But in the "endstate" of the symphony as a whole, Mahler nevertheless transcends Tchaikovskian despair: in the Wagnerian transfiguration of the *Molto adagio*, the putative D major Adagio-Finale slides down a semitone to the redemptive D♭ major "undertonic" in the "true" Adagio-Finale's "deep-throated" swan-song (*à la Tristan*'s C–B transfiguration). The Rondo-Burleske's complicated overlay of previous and endstates may be outlined as follows:

Movement III (Rondo-Burleske) in A minor
A1 (mm. 1–108), including *Fugato* I (mm. 79–108)

B1 (mm. 109–179)
A2 (mm. 180–261), including *Fugato* II (mm. 209–61)
B2 (mm. 262–310)
A3 / *Fugato* III (mm. 311–46)? Becomes a transition to
Movement IV? break-through / Adagio-Finale in D major
  (mm. 347–521) foreshadows the Adagio-Finale in the endstate
  but is undercut by the
"true" A3 (mm. 522–616)
Coda (mm. 617–end)

"True" Movement IV (Adagio) in D♭ major

The Tenth Symphony, which was drafted in the summer of 1910 (i.e. shortly after Mahler had conducted four performances of the *Pathétique* in New York in the spring of that year), might be considered his own *Pathétique*. In terms of surface correlation, funereal elements in the Finale's slow introduction are generically related to the introduction to the *Pathétique*'s first movement and the *Adagio lamentoso*'s coda. At a deeper structural-metaphorical level, Mahler "profoundly integrates" the *Pathétique*'s meta-symphonic sequences as a signifier for inexorable Destiny: if Tchaikovsky's *Pathétique* employs a sequence of descending fifths to represent the "fatal" termination of sequences unleashed in his Symphonies Nos. 4–5 (see Chapter 4), Mahler's Tenth Symphony analogously recomposes and resolves the "fateful" symmetrical sequence initiated in the first movement of the Ninth. Specifically, the sequence of major thirds D – B♭ (second group, m. 80) – F♯ (climax of development, m. 310) – D (recapitulation, m. 347) is recomposed in enlargement across the Tenth Symphony as a whole: F♯ (first and second movements) – B♭ (third movement) – D (tonal goal of the third movement) – F♯ (Finale), and also nested within the Finale itself as D – B♭ (m. 299) – F♯ (m. 315).

In the *Pathétique*'s "failed" *ad astra* narrative, the March is undercut by the *Adagio lamentoso*; the Tenth Symphony's Adagio-Finale "receives" this pathetic "failure" by "crucifying" an "exiled" Sonata-Allegro upon an Adagio Rondo-Finale. Just as Tchaikovsky crucifies himself as homosexual in the *Adagio lamentoso*, in the Adagio-Finale of *his* Tenth, Mahler puts himself as "the Jew" back in the crucified Christ: his comments in the *Particell* reveal the composer representing himself as eternally "exiled" like the "damned" Wandering Jew dancing with the Devil (Fourth Movement: "Der Teufel tanzt es mit mir") and "crucified" like Christ on the Cross (to make this identification clear, Mahler [the Christian convert] actually quotes Christ's words on the Cross: "Erbarmen!! O Gott! O Gott! Warum hast du mich verlassen?" and "Dein Wille geschehe!").[36]

According to normative macro-symphonic form, the first movement should be a sonata form, usually a Sonata-Allegro. (All of the previous Mahler symphonies with the exception of the Fifth conform to this paradigm in various ways.) But in the Tenth Symphony, the expected Sonata-Allegro first movement is displaced by the initial Adagio-Rondo. "Exiled" (like the Wandering Jew) from subsequent movements, in a last-ditch effort to find itself "space" this Sonata-Allegro (mm. 84ff.) "crucifies" itself upon the Adagio Rondo-Finale. But this "crucifixion" of the Sonata-Allegro (programmatically the crucifixion of Mahler as both Wandering Jew *and* Christ) arouses the recapitulatory impulses of super-sonata form: the recapitulation of Christ's climactic "death-scream" and the introduction from the first movement (in mm. 275–98) "liberate" the Adagio-Finale's final strophes for their transfiguration of the opening Adagio. This complicated superimposition of the "failed" Sonata-Allegro on the Rondo-Adagio may be schematized as follows:

Introduction to Movement V: mm. 1–29

First strophe of the Adagio Rondo-Finale: mm. 30–83 ("Pietà Music")

    Superimposed Sonata-Allegro (Mahler's "Jewish" Music)
        Exposition: mm. 84–178
            First group: mm. 84–144
            Second group: mm. 145–78

Second strophe of the Adagio-Rondo occupies space of the development within the Sonata-Allegro (mm. 179–250)

        Recapitulation: mm. 251–74
            Abridged recapitulation of first group: mm. 251–66
            Allusion to second group (mm. 267–74) as transition to

break-through recapitulation of the catastrophic "death scream" and introduction from the first movement smashes the Sonata-Allegro (mm. 275–98) liberating the Adagio-Rondo.

Third strophe of the Adagio-Rondo: mm. 299–314, transition to

Transfigured Recapitulation of First Movement Adagio in the Super-sonata Form
Fourth strophe: mm. 315–51
Fifth strophe: mm. 352–80
Coda: mm. 381–end

Mahler's last valedictory Tenth Symphony "overcomes" the *Pathétique*'s nihilistic pathos by transfiguring Tchaikovsky's *Adagio lamentoso* in a *Pietà*-metaphor. Drawing upon the same iconographic tradition as Michelangelo's Roman *Pietà*, Alma is portrayed as a youthful Mary – *younger* than Her crucified Son; in the Adagio-Rondo's final strophes (as in the Eighth Symphony) she is transfigured as both "Mother and beloved *Bride* of Christ."[37] (In Mahler's meeting with Freud, which took place shortly after the Tenth was drafted, Freud astutely identified Mahler's "Mary-complex."[38]) "Liberated" by the transfiguration of the first movement's Adagio, Mary-as-Alma's post-mortem tenderness reveals her dual nature. The last strophes transmute Tchaikovskian "pathos" into Marian necrophiliac erotic "pity": as in Rilke's 1906 *Pietà*, at the end of the Tenth Symphony, Alma-as-Virgin grieves that she has not slept with Mahler-as-Christ; yet, as in Rilke's poem, both the Virgin and Christ are redeemed as the Virgin cradles the broken Body in her lap:

> But see, Beloved, how your hands are torn –
> Not torn by me, not by my lover's bite.
> Your heart gapes open wide and all may enter
> By that same gate that was to have been mine.
>
> Now are you weary and your weary mouth
> Has no desire unto my bruised lips –
> O Jesus, Jesus, did we miss the hour?
> How wondrously we perish, you and I.[39]

Berg, Britten, and the *Pathétique*'s *Tristan*-deformation

Like Tchaikovsky in the *Pathétique*'s *Adagio lamentoso*, both Berg in *Lulu* and Britten in *Death in Venice* (in *their* valedictory works) associate unhappy and ultimately fatal narratives concerning "sick" homosexual (or lesbian) love with *Tristan*-deformation. Whether either composer was directly influenced by the *Pathétique* remains an open but nonetheless intriguing question. Although I have been unable to document Berg's "exposure" to the *Pathétique*, the Austrian composer was a highly literate musician, and it is improbable that he was unfamiliar with Tchaikovsky's most famous symphony. Britten is known to have studied Tchaikovsky's ballets carefully and to have taken them as models for his own efforts in the genre; he was also familiar with, although apparently less fond of, Tchaikovsky's later symphonies. The Adagio-Finale of Berg's *Lyric Suite*, marked *Largo desolato*, may adopt from the *Pathétique*'s *Adagio lamentoso* both the concept of the macro-symphonic formal deformation (of the Adagio-Finale) and the symbolism of *Tristan*-deformation (through its "profound integration" of the *Tristan* Prelude). Perhaps by deconstructing the *Pathétique*'s homosexual narrative back to its interracial prototype, Berg associates his own "forbidden" passion for the married Jewess Hanna with Baudelaire's "decadent" calenture for the mulatto Jeanne Duval (the "Black Venus").

A possible citation of the "*Tristan* = *Pathétique*" chord associated with tragic lesbianism can be found in the closing music of *Lulu*. Berg identified his lesbian sister Smaragda's "sick disposition" as the cause of her "suffering"; Smaragda provided the model for the Countess Geschwitz, who throughout Acts 2 and 3 "sweats" for Lulu. As the central, tragic figure in the second part of the opera, the Countess – or more specifically her frustrated attraction to Lulu – is associated with the "*Tristan* = *Pathétique*" chord, which is sustained at the climax of the final scene of Act III in the instance when Geschwitz finally recognizes the futility of her pursuit (and Jack-the-Ripper rapes and murders Lulu, mm. 1292–93).[40]

The "*Tristan* = *Pathétique*" chord is similarly associated with tragic homosexuality in Britten's *Death in Venice*, where it represents Aschenbach's unsatisfied homosexual yearning for Tadzio. Roy Travis shows how this chord – which he describes as "that sonic epitome of desire" –

97

conditions the structure of the first and last scenes of Act 1.[41] At the beginning of the opera, Travis observes that "Aschenbach's *Tristan* chord is the goal: he cannot resolve it." Extending Travis's thesis further, it can be shown that the opera's final measures provide the strategically withheld resolution to the "*Tristan = Pathétique*" chord; in other words, the opera as a whole can be interpreted as a colossal structural parody of the *Tristan* Prelude (with the concert ending) whereby the dominant E is finally allowed to resolve to the tonic A major (see the A major conclusion of *Death in Venice*). Perhaps, in the closing scene, Britten also reverses the tragedy of Tchaikovsky's *Adagio lamentoso*, transfiguring homosexual pathos in post-mortem resolution of the "dysfunctional" seventh chord.

Shostakovich, Schnittke, and "pathetic" Soviet man

In a letter to his friend Isaak Glickman (July 1960), Shostakovich calls attention to a large number of quotations in his Eighth String Quartet, including a "hint" of "the second theme from the first movement of Tchaikovsky's Sixth Symphony."[42] Although he does not locate the reference in the score, Shostakovich is probably referring to the first violin's descending sixth e^2–g^1 at Rehearsal 5 in the first movement as a reference to the sixth $f\sharp^2$–a^1 in the Tchaikovsky (mm. 89–90). The quartet seems to be a bitterly ironic parody of Tchaikovskian grand tragedy, which Shostakovich describes as a "pseudo-tragedy . . . so great that, while composing it, my tears flowed as abundantly as urine after downing half a dozen beers."[43] Through the references to the *Pathétique*, the revolutionary song "Tormented by Grievous Bondage" (fourth movement, Rehearsal 58) and Nazi extermination of the Jews ("Jewish" melody from the Second Piano Trio, second movement, Rehearsal 21), in this "autobiographical" quartet, Shostakovich paints his self-portrait as a "pathetic" Soviet Christ.[44] More specifically, the "hint" of the idyllic Tchaikovskian "love" theme conjures an unattainable utopia ironically compromised by oppressive reality.

Perhaps the Shostakovich symphony most closely related to the *Pathétique* is his Ninth (1945). One might not suspect this because the symphony seems to be a buoyant, cheerful piece – at least on the surface. Nor (unlike the Eighth Quartet) does it directly quote the *Pathétique*.

But its *Adagio lamentoso* – its bassoon recitative in the fourth movement – is not fully dispelled by its jaunty victory "March" in the "tacked on," "extra" fifth movement – the putatively triumphant Finale – which upon closer inspection, might be construed as Pyrrhic. How could Shostakovich indulge in such tongue-in-cheek Haydnesque parody when all Stalin wanted was to savor his triumph? Shostakovich himself observes that

> I confess that I gave hope to the leader and teacher's dreams. I announced that I was writing an apotheosis. I was trying to get them off my back but it turned against me. When my Ninth was performed, Stalin was incensed. He was deeply offended, because there was no chorus, no soloists. And no apotheosis.[45]

The Soviet musicologist Boris Asafiev construed "the Ninth as a personal insult," for it is indeed, like the *Pathétique*, a "pathetic" anti-Ninth – a "revocation."[46] But the "*Pathétique*" in Shostakovich's Ninth is essentially *unspoken* if not obliquely articulated being defined more by what the piece is not than what it is; in Shostakovich's *Pathétique*, like Tchaikovsky's, the discourse must be reconstructed from the clues.

That Tchaikovskian "pathos" dogs the steps of Schnittke's compositional personae has not passed without notice in the literature. Schnittke's biographer Ivan Ivashkin, drawing on the composer's own remarks, calls attention to the importance of the *Pathétique*:

> Never before in musical history had there been such a slow finale of such bitter, deep and open pessimism as that of Tchaikovsky's Sixth Symphony. The completion of a structural and logical formation had always been the most important function of the conclusion of a symphony, ensuring the closure of its microcosm. From Tchaikovsky onwards we see the beginning of the tradition of the "indirect" or "false" finale: Tchaikovsky rules out the idea of a final triumph in his Fifth, and in the Sixth altogether refuses to complete the symphony as such. The very idea of the finale collapses. "The finale, which might have explained everything, no longer exists," Schnittke has said. "A finale like the one in Tchaikovsky's Sixth Symphony appears in an age of atheism, when the certainty of belief in God has been lost."[47]

The adagio finale is of great significance for Schnittke, who employs it in a symphonic context in his Third through Fifth and Eighth symphonies, and in his works in other genres as well (in this, he follows Mahler as well as Tchaikovsky). Perhaps it is not coincidental that the symphony by Schnittke which seems closest to the *Pathétique* in its pessimism is *his* Sixth Symphony (1993), although it does not conclude with a slow movement. As described by Edward Rothstein, Schnittke's Sixth "seemed so haunted by death it already seemed to have undergone decay."[48] Like Tchaikovsky's *Pathétique*, Rothstein aptly observes that "its [the Schnittke symphony's] energies are directed at dismantling the very idea of the symphony." At rehearsal 23ff. (mm. 220ff.) in the first movement, Ronald Weitzman specifically connects the striking registral disintegration into the lowest register of the brass and contrabasses with the end of the *Pathétique*: "The shattered remnants [of the orchestra] sound like supplications . . . These pleas reach a level of crying intensity before the instrumental texture (double basses at the same time bolstering and softening the sound of three horns) collapses into a state that Tchaikovsky made indelible in everyone's musical consciousness as his own Sixth Symphony reaches its nadir."[49]

Fascist (mis?)interpretation

Perhaps it is one of the supreme ironies of reception history that the *Pathétique* – a work representing Tchaikovsky's homosexual *grande passion* – should have become a cultural icon of the officially anti-homosexual Third Reich. But perhaps not. It may be that the *Pathétique*'s Nazi interpreters, espousing their own brand of "Nordic-Greek" homosexuality, correctly intuited the significance of Tchaikovsky's late nineteenth-century homosexual battle imagery and made it their own.

In his biography of Herbert von Karajan, Robert C. Bachmann speaks of "facticide" – i.e. the post-war "murder" of the facts – by many prominent conductors active in the Third Reich, including Karajan, Wilhelm Furtwängler, Willem Mengelberg, and Richard Strauss, to name just a few who, after the war, denied their profound engagement with Nazism.[50] But in spite of post-war denials and excuses (still echoed by loyal apologists today), many of these artists were as deeply involved in Nazi cultural propaganda efforts as it was possible to be, and used – or "misused" – Tchaikovsky's *Pathétique* for political and ideological purposes.

In this section, I will focus on interpretations from the late thirties and early forties as "political improvisations"; in other words, I shall suggest that details of performance practice may be directly connected with political circumstances surrounding the performance and the conductor's own political orientation and sympathies. While Karajan, Furtwängler, and Mengelberg were not rabid anti-Semites, they were nevertheless – to varying degrees – sympathetic to fundamental planks of the Nazi platform. That these super-star conductors were attracted to the ideology of the Leader, i.e. to the *Führer*-principle, should not come as a surprise since they were autocrats in their own spheres. Of the above-named, Karajan's ideological affinity to Nazism seems the most clear-cut and unequivocal, and is revealed by his actions, e.g. his voluntary decision to join the Party first in Salzburg on 8 April 1933 and then again in Ulm (Germany) on 1 May 1933 – not in 1935 in order to hold the conducting post at Aachen (as he later falsely claimed).

Furtwängler's and Mengelberg's attitudes to Nazism were more complicated and equivocal, combining accommodation with resistance. Both were relatively unsympathetic to the Nazis' virulent anti-Semitism and saved the lives of a number of Jewish musicians and colleagues. Furtwängler, in particular, is not without influential scholarly apologists like Fred Prieberg, who have portrayed him as a reluctant collaborator.[51] But a more convincing case has been made by those critics who, on balance, accuse Furtwängler of being "a loyal servant of the regime." Michael Kater observes that at a meeting on 28 February 1935, Furtwängler and Goebbels "ironed out their differences and arrived at a new *modus vivendi* . . .":

Many of his [Furtwängler's] future performances were to take place within highly propagandistic frameworks, rendering his art eminently political. Among the first of these, ironically, was his directing Wagner's *Die Meistersinger* at the same party rally that ushered in the anti-Jewish Nuremberg Race Laws of September 1935 – an action on the part of Furtwängler that made a mockery of his broad pledge to save Jews . . . In 1942, after Furtwängler's tour to Scandinavia, Goebbels noted that he was "overflowing with national enthusiasm." Two years later the minister remarked that "the tougher things become, the closer he moves to our regime." What is more, "Furtwängler shows himself from his best side. He is a genuine patriot and warm adherent and advocate of our politics and

101

martial leadership. All one has to do these days is to tell him what one wants from him and he will immediately deliver."[52]

During the occupation, Mengelberg earned the enmity of many Dutch compatriots through his collaborationist relationship with the puppet government leader Seyss-Inquart, and his extensive concertizing in Germany and other European countries under the auspices of the Nazi propaganda organization "Kraft durch Freude." Interestingly, Mengelberg was able to persuade the Dutch and German authorities to let him perform Tchaikovsky's *Pathétique* during the war, *after* the invasion of Russia when German conductors had ceased to conduct it; he was even allowed to record it for Telefunken in April 1941.[53] How Mengelberg got permission to perform an "enemy" composer in 1944 remains mysterious.

As a live art, music may be closely linked with contemporary politics, and, to varying degrees, the interpretations of these conductors are political improvisations responding to contemporary events. Indeed, the idea of Art for Art's sake, i.e. that Art is apolitical, a hypothesis popular during the post-war period of denial and obfuscation, was untenable in the Third Reich (and also in Communist and Western democratic countries, which put their own spins on classical music). From 1933 to 1945, interpretations of classical music were considered part and parcel of the Reich's ideological and political life; contemporary events were made to resonate loudly in choices of program and interpretation. This close connection between art and politics was underscored by Goebbels, who observed:

> The artist undeniably has the right to call himself non-political in a period when politics consists of nothing but shouting matches between parliamentary parties. But at this moment when politics is writing a national drama, when a world is being overthrown – in such a moment the artist cannot say: "That doesn't concern me." It concerns him a great deal.[54]

In this context, the conductor's selection of program and performers, and his interpretative decisions, all have political and ideological overtones: according to Nazi semiotics, the signifier could be a classical composition and the signified a contemporary political event. For example, Karajan could celebrate the *Anschluss* as an act of "liberation" with a performance of *Fidelio* – Beethoven's "rescue" opera being described in the accompanying publicity as a "monumental work of liberation" – in Aachen on 15 April 1938. (Aachen also was of political significance as an "outpost" of the Reich.) Interestingly, this operatic signifier could work both ways: Bruno Walter's volcanic 22 February 1941 performance of *Fidelio* in New York (with Kirsten Flagstad as Leonore) is supercharged with the passion of the émigré hoping to liberate the "good" Germany – and Beethoven, for that matter – from the Nazis.

Given this semiotic relationship between classical music and politics, it is illuminating to examine the recorded interpretations of the *Pathétique* by Karajan, Furtwängler, and Mengelberg. Under their batons in the late thirties and early forties, the *Pathétique*'s March becomes an emblem of resurgent Germany's spiritual–political "rebirth" and apparently limitless capacity for conquest and expansion. The *Adagio lamentoso*, with its connotations of "the slow death of the hero" (as Laroche had described it), accords perfectly with the Nazi cult of the fallen warrior-hero, the *Kamerad* – and without sacrificing the original's homosexual overtones. In view of Tchaikovsky's indigenous militaristic metaphors for Pan-Slavism and triumphant homosexuality discussed in Chapter 4, these fascist "improvisations" might not be misinterpretations at all but extensions of the composer's original intentions. Moreover, Nazi performances of the *Pathétique*'s March may be fruitfully compared with contemporaneous fascist readings of the *Alla marcia* from Beethoven's Ninth Symphony, "Froh, froh, wie seine Sonnen fliegen." In the Nazi context, both the Tchaikovsky and Beethoven marches become metaphors for world–dominating male virility, homosexual bonding, politically reactionary revolution, and chauvinistic militarism. While it is impossible to "prove" this assertion empirically, one senses in Nazi performances of the *Pathétique*'s March and Beethoven's *Alla marcia* a topical connection with the *Einmarsch* to world domination – the breaking down of all norms and boundaries, both political and sexual, and escape into a Dionysiac orgy.[55]

And if, as Goebbels insisted, art and politics were to be inseparably connected, this semantic connotation underlies the studio recordings of the *Pathétique* made by Furtwängler (1938) and Karajan (1939) with the Berlin Philharmonic. Such duplication is noteworthy when one considers the technical limitations of recording on shellac disks and consequently the relatively few studio recordings made by both conductors at that time. (Robert Layton describes this particular duplication as "unprecedented."[56]) Nor does it simply indicate a conductors' competition (although the intense rivalry between Goering's and Goebbels' protégés was probably a factor as well). Rather, these recordings of the *Pathétique* were produced because of their tremendous propagandistic significance for the Reich's larger political-cultural ambitions; in the interpretations of Germany's two pre-eminent conductors, Tchaikovsky's own personal homosexual narrative in the *Pathétique* could tell a new story: the rise of Nazi Germany from the ashes of Weimar, and the reemergence of Teutonic/Nordic ancient Greek heroism and "true" European – i.e. Russian-German – musical culture from the political and social chaos and artistic "degeneracy" of Weimar. (In 1938–39, during this period of Hitler–Stalin alliance, it was highly appropriate for a Russian symphony to serve as the vehicle for purveying this message.) It is interesting that modern critical opinion of Furtwängler's recordings from the Nazi period regards these as his best, without considering whether these interpretations are morally contaminated by their political subtexts. If, in the visual arts, Nazi production has been widely dismissed as *Kitsch*, critical evaluation of Furtwängler's Nazi performances has simply sidestepped the moral issues involved; hiding behind the Art for Art's sake argument, it has simply asserted the intrinsic artistic quality of the product.[57]

The thirty-year-old Karajan's studio recording of the *Pathétique* immediately strikes one as the most fanatically "Nazi" of all. Shortly before making the studio recording, Karajan had conducted a performance of the *Pathétique* in Berlin with the Philharmonic (on 14 March 1939). It elicited rapturous contemporary reviews. For example, in his review for the magazine *Signale zur Musik*, the Berlin critic Alfred Birgfeld singled out Karajan's performance of the March as especially worthy of praise as "that fulminating 'Cossacks' Victory March,'" which had "formed an unimaginable, rousing climax."[58] Karajan's recording seems to relive the Third Reich's self-mythologized history. The symphony's "painful" introduction, with which Tchaikovsky had reopened the homosexual "wound" of the Fifth Symphony, is revalued through its exaggeratedly slow tempo to depict the "darkness" of Germany's great "need" during the early thirties: in the tortured introduction, the listener is brought face to face with not only the Great Depression, the mass unemployment, inflation, and social unrest, but the birth pangs of the "New" Germany. In the first group, "darkness" is redemptively illuminated by focused "light" (one is reminded here of the Nazi "spiritual" light shows): a "new" sun rises – a sun sealed with the imprimatur of the swastika and the slogan "Deutschland erwache!" ("Germany arise") familiar from banners and emblazoned on postcards of German towns back-lit by this Nazi star. Karajan's emphatic articulation of the rising fourths as "a call to battle" in the first group (upper strings, mm. 43ff.) is clearly intended to foreshadow the triumphant fourths in the March, which he then takes at break-neck speed (8′03″ compared to Furtwängler's already fast 9′12″ and his own later recordings, all of which take longer than his 1939 performance).[59] In the first movement's deliberately "over-blown" climax (mm. 285ff.) the conductor seems to invoke none other than the heroic Leader himself.

Made shortly after Germany had invaded the rest of Czechoslovakia, Karajan's recording of the March is tinged with the resonances of *Einmarsch* (Germany invaded the Sudetenland in October 1938). Through carefully shaped yet exaggerated dynamic wedges, through dynamic growth and gradual tonal focus, Karajan, Furtwängler, and Mengelberg, each in their own way, recreate the "New Germany's" inexorable advance. In these readings of the March, the listener confronts the musical realization of Leni Riefenstahl's "Triumph of the Will" and the struggle to victory – in the triumph of the March theme in G major, the listener is again compelled to hail the *Führer* and the conquests of the "New Germany." The significance of these connotations was certainly not lost on the record companies (in terms of potential record sales), the Propaganda Ministry, and contemporary audiences. One detects in Karajan's jaunty yet astonishingly clipped, guttural articulation of the triumphant arrival of the March theme echoes of the Nazi pop music that he was conducting at the time. Karajan himself would soon eagerly participate in the *Einmarsch* of "victorious" German culture; sentiments of advance and conquest resonate in a speech he gave to the Berlin Philharmonic prior to its 1940 "tour" of occupied Holland, Belgium, and France:

The great German masters of music have expressed in their music what we are trying to realize in the visible world. Thus we might say that a common responsibility to the great masters connects us with those who have the most difficult task and the decisive role in the construction of the New Germany: the men of our incomparable Wehrmacht.[60]

If Mengelberg's sympathies lay with a resurgent Germany – even after the invasion of Holland – they seem to be articulated in his 1941 recording of the *Pathétique*. Though less extreme in its tempi, and arguably more musical in its sensitivity to detail and balance than Karajan's interpretation, one senses in Mengelberg's reading the same fascination with Nazism that had enthralled so many collaborationists. Of course, one could argue, no doubt with justification, that Mengelberg had a long association with Tchaikovsky, which he was merely continuing, albeit under difficult circumstances. He had first conducted the *Pathétique* with the Concertgebouw in the 1897/98 season; shortly thereafter, he had conducted Tchaikovsky's music in Russia, and through his friendship with Modest, gained access to what he believed (falsely in the event) were Tchaikovsky's final revisions (these *retouches* can be heard in his recordings). But then Mengelberg also had been even more profoundly engaged with Mahler, whose music he had been prepared to abandon – and rather too readily. In a letter of March 1943 from "some old Concertgebouw friends," Mengelberg is chastised for having "deserted country, city and orchestra in the years of greatest trials in order to chase after your own personal success and – in a safe place enjoy a rest that you could not enjoy in dignity, disturbed as it would have been by the appearance of Mahler and the others whose friendship you have betrayed."[61]

The Karajan, Furtwängler, and Mengelberg interpretations of the *Pathétique*'s *Adagio lamentoso* are especially fascinating on account of Nazism's complicated attitude to homosexuality. Because of the vogue of the ancient Greek, heroic and homosexual themes tended to blend in Nazi ideology and art, converging on the homosexual warrior. Although the Nazi Party had advocated a hard line towards homosexuals even during the Weimar Republic, Hitler had initially defended the openly homosexual Ernst Röhm, the ex-soldier chief of the Storm Troopers and his coterie of homosexuals in the upper echelons of the SA, saying that Röhm's private life was his own affair as long as he exercised some discretion. (One might argue that Röhm's clique of SA homosexuals embodied precisely that kind of militaristic male bonding which Tchaikovsky had celebrated in the *Pathétique*'s March and *Adagio lamentoso*.) In the "Night of the Long Knives" in 1934, Röhm and his "friends" were liquidated for sedition rather than their homosexual proclivities, although Hitler later justified their murder by referring obliquely to "moral corruption." But even after the homophobic Himmler's systematic persecution of homosexuals had begun in earnest, the ideology and imagery of homosexuality nevertheless continued to flourish in Nazi art.

In Nazi interpretations of the *Pathétique*'s *Adagio lamentoso*, Tchaikovsky's homosexual lament in the Finale is transfigured (in a characteristically Nazi synthesis of Greek and Catholic symbolism) as a homosexual *Pietà* for the fallen warrior "friend" – the *Kamerad* (notice the cruciform symbolism in Arno Breker's 1939 relief *Kameradschaft* for a monument in Berlin [see Plate 3, p. 109]). At the root of this Nazi *topos* was ancient "heroic" homosexuality, going back to the "comradeship" (*Kameradschaft*) of the Greek warriors: for example, in the *Iliad*, Achilles is described as mourning the death of his beloved Patroclus with grief so extreme that even Zeus and Athena were moved to pity.

The early Nazi movement also gleaned inspiration from the homosexual poet Stefan George's idealization of his boy-love Maximin, who had died young in 1905 and became for George a symbol of heroic youth, the flower of what he called the "secret Germany" of the future. In many respects, George's circle foreshadowed Röhm's. He picked his disciples for their looks and prophesied that a new Leader would surround himself with ideal male beauties (like Maximin) to guard the "secret Germany" until the Reich could be reborn in their image. In deference to Greek models, the Nazis even tinged heterosexual relationships with homosexual connotations, the ideal sportive *Kameradin* being the boyishly flat-chested female, as depicted in many films, photographs, sculptures, and paintings from the period. In spite of Röhm's dire fate, the ideological theorists, artists, conductors, and critics of the Third Reich never eradicated the homosexual content inherited from their Greek models; rather, they discovered that by inflating this *topos* to grandiose and "heroic" proportions it could become appropriately "chaste." For example, the two monumental muscular young men in Joseph Thorak's *Kameradschaft* for the German Pavillon at the 1937 International Exposition in Paris discreetly hold hands (see Plate 2). Although their hands

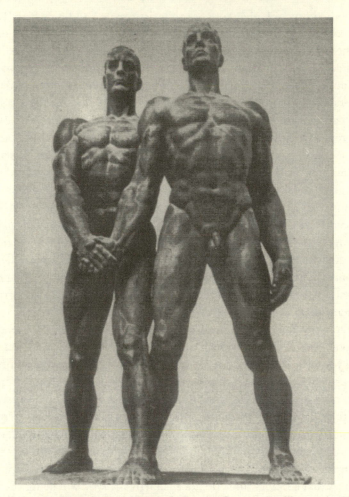

Plate 2 Joseph Thorak, *Kameradschaft*. For the German Pavilion at the 1937
International Exhibition in Paris

clasp over the genitals of one of the men and their legs gently touch, such
gestures are justified as suggesting the manly virility of these Nordic-
Greek defenders of the Aryan race. If the "chastity" of their relationship
is subtly belied by these gestures, their idealized nakedness depicts the
Kameradschaft of "blond beasts" fighting to preserve Western civiliza-
tion. Perhaps it is not insignificant that in 1936 in Aachen, Karajan pro-

Plate 3 Arno Breker, *Kameradschaft*, 1939

duced a cantata for choir and orchestra by the otherwise unknown Nazi composer Heinrich Gemacher called *Kameradschaft*.[62]

Passion – and grief – is in evidence in Breker's *Kameradschaft* (Breker was one of Hitler's favorite sculptors, Plate 3). Interestingly, the martial context of the beloved youth's death remains entirely implicit; explicit only is the older warrior's distress (this relief bears a remarkable resemblance to Broc's *Death of Hyacinth*, Plate 1, discussed in Chapter 1). The "chastely" inflated homosexual pathos of Breker's design closely parallels analogously "monumental" contemporary readings of the *Adagio lamentoso* as laments for the fallen warrior. Another dimension that "purifies" the homosexual element in the lament is its relation to the cult of the fallen soldier as it developed in Germany after the First World War. As George Mosse observes,

> The memory of the war was refashioned into a sacred experience which provided the nation with a new depth of religious feeling, putting at its disposal ever-present saints and martyrs, places of worship, and a heritage to emulate. The picture of the fallen soldier in the arms of Christ, so common during and after the First World War, projected the traditional belief in martyrdom and resurrection onto the nation as an all-encompassing civic religion. The cult of the fallen soldier became a centerpiece of the religion of nationalism after the war, having its greatest political impact in nations like Germany which had lost the war and had been brought to the edge of chaos by the transition from war to peace.[63]

The Nazis identified their own martyrs with the cult of the fallen warrior; for example, the young Nazi Preiser, who fell in street fights in 1932, was reputed to have said as he died "My father fell in the service of Germany. I as his son can do no less." "Unprecedented" Nazi interest in the *Pathétique* is no less related to the battle and conquest imagery of the March than the pathos of the fallen warrior as depicted in the *Adagio lamentoso*. But, in Nazi interpretations of the *Pathétique*, the homosexual dimension of the *topos* of the dead *Kamerad* was not completely obscured. For example, in his book on Furtwängler published in 1940, the Nazi critic Friedrich Herzfeld circumspectly – yet directly – alludes to Tchaikovsky's tragic homosexual passion as his "tragically lost humanity," which he hears lurking behind Furtwängler's "enormous" (*ungeheuer*) interpretation:

> In his interpretation of the *Pathétique*, we come closest to the program, which serves as a human-poetic background to Tchaikovsky's music, even though, admittedly, it cannot be described by words and concepts. But we can sense that he [Tchaikovsky] expressed the full tragedy of his aberrant humanity (*verirrten Menschentums*) . . .[64]

The *Pathétique* at the movies: Ken Russell's splice of *Manfred* and the *Pathétique*

Of the four films made on Tchaikovsky to date, the one by Ken Russell is the most interesting from an interpretative point of view, especially in its use of the *Pathétique*.[65] The earliest of these films, *Es war eine rauschende Ballnacht* (Germany 1939), again reflects Nazi fascination with Tchaikovsky. Praised at the time, the film is an erotic fantasy rather distantly related to the facts of Tchaikovsky's life: the composer finds himself caught between a *danseuse*, who loves him, and a society lady, who worships him and secretly furthers his career (obviously modeled on von Meck).

Ken Russell's film *The Music Lovers* (Great Britain 1971), starring Richard Chamberlain as Tchaikovsky and Glenda Jackson as his wife Antonina Milyukova, is (like the German film) a fantasy. However, although the intent is not to create a documentary, this film (like Russell's other films about composers) is imaginatively concerned with painting a psychologically "true" portrait. To give full play to Tchaikovsky's complicated and ambivalent feelings about his homosexuality, Russell focuses upon the 1876–77 marriage crisis, centering the action on the relationship between the composer and his wife. Although Russell conflates and distorts "the facts" the film is nevertheless penetrating. For example, Russell draws a parallel – in my view justly – between Tchaikovsky's unconsummated relationships with Antonina and Nadezhda von Meck suggesting that, although the former proved unbearable, the latter was spiritually fulfilling. Although biographically false, it is nonetheless psychologically telling in this regard that, to strains of the death music from the end of *Romeo and Juliet*, at one point Nadezhda even lies down next to the sleeping Tchaikovsky as if to suggest that they are man and wife – or at least lovers like Romeo and Juliet – who have been tragically prevented from enjoying their love by cruel Destiny. There is something true in this, for there can be no doubt that Tchaikovsky played out a "marriage" of sorts with Nadezhda.

A most striking aspect of the film is Russell's use of music from the *Pathétique*. That he features this piece at all is, of course, anachronistic because the events being represented throughout much of the film concern the 1876–77 Milyukova debacle and the *Pathétique* was only conceived much later; but, for this temporal conflation, the director is not to be faulted. On the contrary, it is essential to the psychological portrait. Poetically, we may allow the composer to "hear ahead" in his life. The music from the Sixth Symphony first appears well into the film at the point when, having had a miserable time on their honeymoon, Tchaikovsky and Antonina precipitously decide to take the night train back to St. Petersburg. In their private sleeping compartment, they become drunk on champagne, and Antonina removes her clothes and attempts to force Tchaikovsky to have intercourse. In some of the shots, Antonina's undone corset appears to be a huge vortex, threatening like a giant vagina to swallow up and devour the unfortunate composer, who, impotent, collapses with horror and bald terror at the sight of feminine pulchritude. It is precisely at this point that Russell injects the music of the development section of the *Pathétique*'s first movement: the director correctly intuits the semantic significance of this passage as a depiction of Hell.

But Russell wishes the "orgy" scene in the train to last longer than the duration of the first movement's development through to the recapitulation of the second group, that is, approximately five minutes. The scene must extend longer because Tchaikovsky's inability to have sex with Antonina and, as importantly, his recognition of his visceral disgust for heterosexual intercourse, are the crux of the film; it must have the appropriate visual and musical weight. However, since it is to go on, Russell finds himself running out of "infernal," agitated music from the *Pathétique*; furthermore, the music's dissipation into the B major recapitulation renders the *Pathétique*'s continuation unusable. Russell's solution to this problem is both ingenious and remarkable, revealing his appreciation of the semantics of Tchaikovsky's music: he splices the coda from the *Manfred* Symphony's outer movements (Tchaikovsky initiates both codas with the same music) onto the end of the *Pathétique*'s development and first group's recapitulation. The result is that the dominant in m. 304 of the *Pathétique* resolves to the tonic in the *Manfred* coda, a solution which is made possible by the fact that *Manfred*, like the *Pathétique*, is in B minor. Russell thereby not only intuits the connection between *Manfred* and the *Pathétique* that was pointed out earlier, but actualizes it. His solution is not only practical –

allowing the scene to continue for several more painful minutes – it is poetic. For those "in the know," it suggests that Tchaikovsky himself "hears ahead" in his career to his self-portrait as a perverse *Manfred* (condemned for his incestuous lust), unable to "perform" "normally" and thereby condemned.

7

Platonic postlude

Although Orlova and her detractors have debated the truth or falsehood of her account of the Court of Honor which, she claimed, condemned Tchaikovsky to take his own life or face exposure as a homosexual, no one has stepped back from the thorny issue of veracity to treat the story simply as part of reception history. But doing this opens up new and interesting perspectives on the reception of Tchaikovsky's life and work. The Orlova story is of considerable interest because of the way it interprets Tchaikovsky as a Socrates-like figure. In 399 BC, three Athenian citizens – Meletus, Anytus, and Lycon – brought public charges against Socrates. He was accused of "heresy" and, more importantly, of "corrupting the minds of the young." There are many parallels between Orlova's Tchaikovsky and Plato's Socrates: both are elderly homosexuals who surround themselves with coteries of adoring young men, both worship beauty and are prepared to sacrifice everything for it and, ultimately, both are forced to commit suicide for "corrupting youth."

But perhaps there is something to this association, even if it proves to be factually incorrect. Valid parallelisms can indeed be drawn between Socrates' and Tchaikovsky's ideas of love as expressed in the Platonic dialogues and the Sixth Symphony. The *Pathetique*'s primary subject is Tchaikovsky's great love for Bob – a love which inspires yet torments and ultimately destroys the lovers. The representation of this terrifying passion in the symphony transforms it into a thing of beauty: as "divine" madness, love becomes the inspiration for art. These ideas, which are integral to both the subject and compositional process of the Sixth Symphony, are remarkably close to Plato's views on homosexual love and the Beautiful as articulated in the *Phaedrus*. In the important discussion of "Love," Plato defines it as "a type of madness, which befalls when a man, reminded by the sight of beauty [in the boy] on earth of the true beauty, grows his wings and endeavors to fly upward, but in vain, exposing himself to the reproach of insanity because like a bird he fixes his gaze on the heights to the neglect of things below." Neither Plato's Socrates nor Orlova's Tchaikovsky is prepared to sacrifice this divine madness to save himself; in the end, each elects to die by taking the poisoned drink. It was Plato's intention to represent Socrates as a martyr, and Orlova's account accomplishes the same thing for Tchaikovsky. Orlova's story meshes nicely with the tragic interpretation of the *Pathétique* as a suicide letter, and as a symphonic "apology" in the spirit of Plato's *Apology*, *Crito*, and *Phaedo*.

Considered as part of contemporary reception history, the harsh reaction of Orlova's critics to her Platonic "spin" can be explained by today's climate: within many artistic and critical disciplines including musicology, it is politically incorrect to problematize Tchaikovsky's homosexuality and death. Until quite recently, political correctness similarly redeemed Mahler as "happy" Jew. For example, in a widely viewed television program on Mahler shot in Israel, Leonard Bernstein simplistically celebrated Mahler as a "Jewish composer." But, as we have seen, Mahler's Jewish – like Tchaikovsky's homosexual – narrative is, to say the least, "problematic." Following Wagner's emphatic advice, and that of other late nineteenth-century anti-Semites (including the Jewish ones), some assimilated, "cultured" Jews decided that the best "solution" to their "Jewish problem" was suicide. Perhaps Orlova's Tchaikovsky too hastily takes this suicidal cue from the contemporary homophobes who – allegedly – sat in secret judgement upon him. But those who try to prettify Tchaikovsky's "negative" view of the consequences of his homosexuality as represented "autobiographically" in his *Pathétique* also do the composer, the music, and the modern discipline of musicology a disservice. Rather, let us acknowledge the existence of Tchaikovsky's "homosexual problem" and sensitively explore its connotations in their full complexity; as interwoven narrative strands in some of the greatest music ever composed, they have become a thing of beauty.

Appendix A

Pathétique, the macro-symphonic structure (middleground views of movements 1–4)

(a) First movement

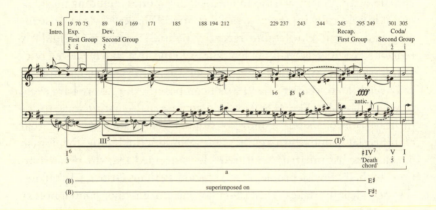

(b) Second movement

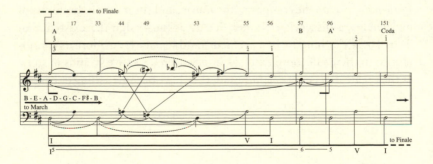

(c) Third movement

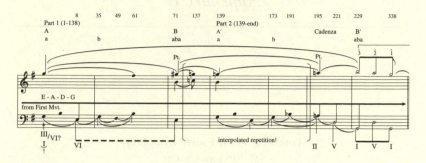

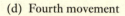

(d) Fourth movement

Appendix B

Tritonality in the Fourth Symphony
(a) First movement

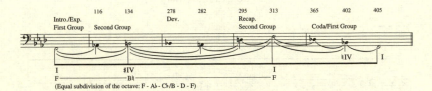

(b) Second movement

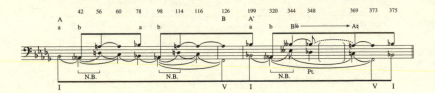

(c) Third movement

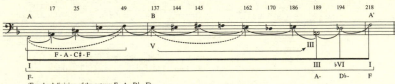

(d) Fourth movement

Appendix C

Tritonality in the Fifth Symphony
(a) First movement

(b) Second movement

(c) Third movement

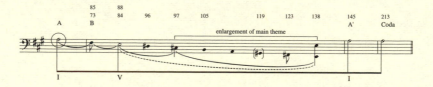

(d) Fourth movement

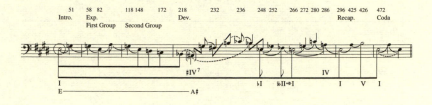

Notes

1 "Pathetic" metaphors for sexuality and race, gambling and destiny

1 Brown, *Tchaikovsky*, vol. IV, p. 443.
2 Brown, vol. IV, p. 444. References to dates follow the Julian calendar (used in Russia until 1918), which was twelve days behind the Western Gregorian calendar. In using the Russian dates for events in Russia, I follow the practice of standard English-language books on Tchaikovsky.
3 For a recent discussion of this issue, cf. Brown, "How Did Tchaikovsky Come to Die?" 581–89.
4 George L. Mosse, *The Creation of Modern Masculinity* (Oxford: Oxford University Press, 1996), p. 80.
5 Cf. my "Sexuality and Structure in Tchaikovsky," pp. 6ff.
6 Modest rejected Hugo Riemann's suggestion that his brother had borrowed the title and the opening motive from Beethoven's *Pathétique*.
7 Orlova (*Tchaikovsky: A Self-Portrait*, p. 333) translates Tchaikovsky's remarks on Beethoven (dating from 1888): "I will begin with Beethoven, whom it is customary to praise without stint and before whom we are ordered to bow down as before God. So, what do I think of Beethoven? I do bow down before the greatness of some of his works, but I do *not love* Beethoven. My attitude to him reminds me of what I used to feel in my childhood about the Lord of *Sabaoth*. He used to fill me with a sense of astonishment and dread at the same time (nor have my feelings changed even now)."
8 McClary, *Carmen*, especially Chapter 3, "Images of Race, Class, and Gender in Nineteenth-Century French Culture," pp. 29–43.
9 Edward Garden (*Tchaikovsky*, p. 148) detects Tchaikovsky's influence on Puccini: "Tchaikovsky's music had some influence on three other highly individual composers who have apparently . . . little in common with each other . . . Puccini, Sibelius and Stravinsky. Puccini is perhaps the most obvious of these. The more tortured moments in the relatively early *Tosca* (1900) and the late *Turandot* (1924), for example, have clear antecedents in *The Queen of Spades* and Tchaikovsky's late symphonies."

10 Whether Bizet was Jewish has been the subject of considerable debate. Gdal Saleski reports (*Famous Musicians of Jewish Origins* [New York: Bloch Publishing Company, 1949], p. 14):

> While preparing my *Famous Musicians of a Wandering Race* (1927), I based my research both on previous documentary publications and on personal contacts. I visited Paris in 1922 and again in 1924, to gather additional material on the lives of French-Jewish composers and musicians. Several persons were interviewed regarding the Jewish ancestry of Bizet. A friend of long standing, Dr. Henri Sliosberg, a renowned lawyer in pre-Soviet Russia, whom I visited several times in Paris, introduced me to an eminent French septuagenarian musicologist who, in his youth, had known Bizet personally. From him I learned that Bizet's maternal grandparents were Spanish Jews. May I also refer you to a book written by Dr. Adolph Kohut, entitled *Berühmte Israelitische Männer und Frauen*, published originally in 1871, in which Bizet's biography and photograph were included . . . In 1892 this volume was translated into several versions, which did not omit Bizet's biography. In view of the fact that Dr. Kohut's book originally appeared during Bizet's lifetime (he died in 1875), and he was at no time thereafter forced to repudiate or retract the statement of the composer's origin, it is safe to assume that Bizet had Jewish blood in his veins . . . In *Das Judenthum in der Musik*, by Simon Levy, Erfurt, 1930, Bizet is described as "ein halb-spanischer Jude."

According to Jewish law, which traces lineage matriarchally, Bizet was Jewish. Interestingly, as Erik Levi observes (*Music in the Third Reich*, [New York: Saint Martin's Press, 1994], p. 192): "Bizet's *Carmen* maintained its popularity in the Third Reich despite a propaganda campaign that sought to place question marks as to the racial origins of its composer." Recordings of *Carmen* were permitted to be sold in Nazi Germany. Interestingly, the Halévys did not consider Bizet Jewish at all and were unhappy with his marriage into their family for precisely this reason. Ruth Jordan reports (*Fromental Halévy, His Life and Music, 1799–1863* [London: Kahn and Averill, 1994], p. 211): "Geneviève, aged fifteen, grew up under the domination of an unstable, self-centred mother. When Bizet and she fell in love and wanted to get married a united Halévy–Rodrigues clan objected to a gentile husband."

11 These potentially redemptive transmutations became an essential part of the semantic language of nineteenth- and twentieth-century music. For this reason, later in the twentieth century, European and American Jewish composers would employ the less threatening Blacks as metaphors or tropes – or, from a semiotic perspective, as signifiers – for themselves. Tchaikovsky's racially schizophrenic Odette-Odile is dignified and made socially acceptable through her metamorphosis into a "white-black" swan, just as Meyerbeer's persecuted but redeemed Jews become Africans and Huguenots (as later

gured as Southern Blacks).

12 Other painters associated with David whose work has homosexual overtones include Anne Louis Girodet (1767–1824, a man), Pierre Narcisse Guérin (1774–1833), and Claude Marie Dubufe (1790–1864).

13 In the scientific literature of Tchaikovsky's time, homosexuals were described as "buggers," "perverts," and "inverts"; see Greenberg, *The Construction of Homosexuality*.

14 Ibid., p. 400.

15 This causal linkage between Carmen's questioning of Destiny through the oracle of the cards and her murder was made even more explicit in the first version of the opera's conclusion (*redundantly* obvious in Bizet's later view): in the original version, after she had been stabbed but before she expired, Carmen made a gesture of cutting the cards. Bizet even allowed her to speak in a monotone as she died imitating the earlier oracular pronouncement of the cards (in eight subsequently cut and now-lost measures, he interpolated a transformation of text and music from the card-divination scene in Act 2). For the earlier versions of the ending in so far as it has survived in the manuscripts see Fritz Oeser, *Georges Bizet, Carmen. Kritische Neuausgabe nach den Quellen* (Kassel, 1964), pp. 840–47.

16 One of the many issues debated in the recent literature concerns the enigmatic allusions to emotions encrypted in the symbols "X" and "Z" in the diary. Most commentators have interpreted these designations as coded references to the composer's homosexual urges. Noting that "X" and "Z" almost always occur in the context of references to games of vint and gambling, Poznansky has proposed that these letters may also refer to emotions emanating from the card-game vint (a Russian form of bridge).

2 Background and early reception

1 See Poznansky, *The Quest for the Inner Man*, pp. 556–57; Holden, *Tchaikovsky*, p. 332.

2 Poznansky, *Tchaikovsky's Last Days*, pp. 27–28.

3 Holden, *Tchaikovsky*, p. 333.

4 Foreword to the Sikorski pocket score of the Symphony in E♭, 1961.

5 Holden, *Tchaikovsky*, p. 333.

6 Foreword to the Sikorski edition of the Symphony in E♭.

7 Poznansky, *Tchaikovsky's Last Days*, p. 63.

8 Holden, *Tchaikovsky*, p. 333.

9 Kraus, "Tchaikovsky," p. 321. It is possible that the original "Life" program *per se* – but *not* the musical ideas associated with it – eventually "bifurcated"

into *both* the first three movements of the *Pathétique* and the final version of the E♭ Major Piano Concerto (after the symphonic version of the E♭ music had been rejected). Accordingly, the first movement of the Concerto might represent "Youth," the second movement "Love," and the third movement "Struggle and Victory," as has been proposed recently by pianist-musicologist Andrei Hoteyev ("Tchaikovsky Reconsidered: Andrei Hoteev Talks to Martin Anderson," *Fanfare* 22/4 (March 1999), pp. 74–92). Regarding Hoteyev's suggestion that Tchaikovsky intended the optimism of the E♭ Major Concerto to counterbalance the pessimism of the *Pathétique*, this hypothesis overlooks the fact that Tchaikovsky tore up the symphonic version of the E♭ major music, violently "banishing" it from the symphonic narrative. By "exiling" this optimistic music to a different, peripheral genre, it is clear that he did *not* wish it to participate in the symphonic discourse and thereby mitigate the overwhelming pessimism of that narrative (see pp. 71–73). However, Hoteyev does provide important new information about the piano concertos as a whole and the last works for piano and orchestra in particular.

10 Brown, *Tchaikovsky*, vol. IV, p. 443. Poznansky in *Tchaikovsky's Last Days*, p. 27, gives different dates, stating that the sketch was completed by 24 March and orchestrated between 19 July and 19 August.

11 It is believed that Tchaikovsky played through the symphony in the two-piano arrangement with Lev Konyus.

12 Pozansky, *Tchaikovsky's Last Days*, p. 58.

13 Volkov, *Balanchine's Tchaikovsky*, pp. 219–20.

14 Holden, *Tchaikovsky*, p. 345.

15 Poznansky, *Tchaikovsky's Last Days*, p. 27.

16 Ibid., p. 27.

3 Form and large-scale harmony

1 Kraus, "Tchaikovsky," p. 300.

2 Holden, *Tchaikovsky*, pp. 332–33.

3 For some recent studies of sonata deformation see Hepokoski, *Sibelius. Symphony No. 5*; Warren Darcy, "Bruckner's Sonata Deformations," in *Bruckner Studies*, ed. Timothy L. Jackson and Paul Hawkshaw (Cambridge: Cambridge University Press, 1997), pp. 256–77; and Jackson, "The Finale of Bruckner's Seventh Symphony."

4 The two works by Tchaikovsky exhibiting this form, the *Tempest Overture* (1873) and the first movement of the Fourth Symphony, are analyzed in detail in my 1995 "Sexuality and Structure in Tchaikovsky." There, I noted the generic relationship of this kind of partial reversal to "break-through"

technique, observing that "The brief, climactic appearance of the first theme at the climax of the development in both the *Tempest* and the Fourth Symphony is generically related to what James Hepokoski calls a 'break-through deformation,' this being defined as 'an unforeseen inbreaking of a seemingly new . . . event in or at the close of the "development space," [which] typically renders a normative . . . recapitulation invalid.'"

5 Cf. Hepokoski's discussion of "Durchbruch" in "Strauss's *Don Juan* Revisited," p. 142.

6 Tchaikovsky already employs the break-through technique in the outer movements of his First Symphony (1866, revised 1874). The sonata form of the first movement eloquently reveals the composer's penchant for unorthodox formal-harmonic thinking. The exposition (mm. 1–250) is subdivided into a first group (mm. 1–67), an extended bridge (mm. 68–136), and a second group (mm. 137–250) following "textbook" sonata models. The second group, however, is remarkable for its harmonic freedom within the dominant prolongation and its break-through-like interpolation (mm. 162–210) – a passage which is not recomposed in the recapitulation. The break-through also figures prominently in the First Symphony's Finale. The introduction, which makes reference to the first movement (mm. 1–64), leads to a brilliant first group (mm. 65–88); a *fugato* bridge section (mm. 89–125) introduces the chorale-like second group (mm. 126–200). A terse, contrapuntal development (mm. 201–81) culminates in the recapitulation of the first group (mm. 282–304). The reprise of the *fugato* bridge section (mm. 305–42) intimates the recapitulation of the second group; but, at this point (mm. 343ff.), the recapitulation deforms the normative sonata form paradigm: instead of the expected reprise of the second group, a ghostly allusion to the second subject (mm. 343–58) is transformed into a break-through recall of the introduction (mm. 359–66), introducing a remarkable, extended chromatic fantasy (mm. 367–414) based on augmentations of the descending figure from the second subject. Only in m. 415 is the second group released as an apotheosis of the chorale theme. In terms of the larger narrative, the role of the "meditative" chromatic fantasy is to prepare the protagonist for the final, redeeming revelation. Thus, the *ad astra* redemption-metaphor, thwarted in the first movement, can be fulfilled in the last.

7 In the context of *Manfred*'s super-sonata symphonic form, its Finale bears a double recapitulatory burden: the Finale's recapitulatory obligations include reprising its own sonata's first and second groups along with those of the first movement (in conformance with the super-sonata idea). Tchaikovsky solves this problem by employing no fewer than three recapitulatory spaces. As in normative sonata form, the exposition is divided into first (mm. 1–80) and second groups (mm. 81–160), a transformed reminiscence of Manfred's

material (mm. 161–205) from the beginning of the first movement rounding out the exposition. The development section (mm. 206–66) is a double fugue based on the principal themes of the Finale's first and second groups, which is brought to a close (like the exposition) with a reminiscence of *Manfred*'s opening (mm. 267–81). The first recapitulation (mm. 282–302) reprises the Finale's first theme combined with Manfred's theme from the first movement; the second recapitulation (mm. 337–93) reprises the Astarte material, which had been omitted from the recapitulation in the first movement, while the third recapitulation (mm. 394–end) presents a transfigured recapitulation of the first movement's reprise of Manfred's music, the strong parallelism between the conclusions of the outer movements reinforcing the effect of super-sonata symphonic form.

8 Quoted from Timothy L. Jackson, "Diachronic Transformation in a Schenkerian Context. A Study of the Brahms Haydn Variations Op. 56a-b," in *Schenker Studies 2*, ed. Hedi Siegel and Carl Schachter (Cambridge: Cambridge University Press, 1999).

9 In other words, in the *Pathétique*, the normative sequence of movements in the standard paradigm of macro-symphonic form is deformed – i.e. "interrupted" and rearranged – through a formal *peripety* so as to undercut the *ad astra* narrative established in the Fourth and Fifth Symphonies. This "tragic" movement-reversal is generically related to the group-reversal in the "tragic" reversed recapitulation (cf. Jackson, "Tragic Reversed Sonata Form").

10 According to sonata form convention, both the exposition and recapitulation should begin on the tonic chord in root position, a paradigm which Tchaikovsky follows in his first three symphonies. In the first movements of Symphonies 1–5, and "7," the sonata exposition opens firmly on the tonic. The First Symphony unfurls a pseudo-folk melody against the backdrop of a stable tonic tremolo. The Second and Third Symphonies each begin with extended introductions, which prolong the dominants of their main keys in the manner of Haydn, Mozart, and Beethoven; in both of these symphonies, however, the prolonged dominant in the introductions resolves strongly to the root position tonic at the onset of the sonata form proper. The introductions to the Fourth and Fifth Symphonies both open firmly on the tonic, as do their sonata expositions. The E♭ Major "Seventh" Symphony, which does not feature an introduction, emphatically opens on its tonic. In the first movements of Symphonies Nos. 1–3, the structural recapitulation reasserts the tonic (First Symphony, m. 40; Second Symphony, m. 220; Third Symphony, m. 308).

11 I distinguish between "design" coda and "structural" coda. The "design" of a composition is its motivic-thematic substance; the "structure" is its tonal

organization. The distinction between design and structure was first made by Felix Salzer in *Structural Hearing* (New York: Charles Boni, 1952) and has since been widely adopted in the Schenkerian literature. The "design" coda generally occurs after the "design" of the exposition has been fully represented in the recapitulation; the structural coda usually begins after the fundamental line (the Schenkerian *Urlinie*) has descended to the tonic. Usually the design and structural codas are initiated simultaneously. In other words, the recapitulation of the design is realized so that its termination coincides with the definitive resolution of the structural upper voice (on $\hat{1}$). But in the Tchaikovsky, the design coda and structural coda are "out of phase." As shown in Appendix A, ex. a, the fundamental line is undivided, the structural descent continuing through the recapitulation of the first group by eliminating the expected interruption (on $\hat{2}$) at the beginning of the reprise. Since the fundamental line definitively descends to $\hat{1}$ in the recapitulation of the second group, the structural coda *anticipates* the design coda. In my analysis of the Finale of Brahms's Third Violin Sonata Op. 108 ("The Tragic Reversed Recapitulation in the German Classical Tradition," *Journal of Music Theory* 40 [1996]), pp. 85–88), I show how, in this piece, the structural coda also precedes the design coda; design similarly outpaces structure. I observe that "these design–structural 'misunderstandings' may be part of the purely musical tragedy embodied in this impassioned work." Similarly, the first movement of the *Pathétique* embodies a tragic design–structure "misunderstanding."

12 Volkov, *Balanchine's Tchaikovsky*, p. 120.

4 The "not-so-secret" program – a hypothesis

1 Poznansky, *The Quest for the Inner Man*, p. 559.

2 Ibid.

3 Solomon Volkov, *Testimony. The Memoirs of Dmitri Shostakovich* (New York: Harper and Row, 1979; repr. 1990), p. 235. The work of reconstructing the texts of Tchaikovsky's censored letters has been undertaken by V. Sokolov, and is presented in *P. I. Tchaikovsky: Forgotten and New Reminiscences of Contemporaries, New Materials and Documents*, ed. Vaidman and Belonovich (Moscow, 1995). In "Unknown Tchaikovsky: A Reconstruction of Previously Censored Letters to His Brothers (1875–79)," in *Tchaikovsky and His World*, ed. Kearney, pp. 55–98, Poznansky is nebulous regarding whether his English translations are based on his own reconstructions or are simply translations of those published by Sokolov. But, if anything, the uncensored letters as presented in Poznansky's translations reveal the depth of

Tchaikovsky's anxiety, confusion, and distress concerning his homosexuality in the late 1870s and do not advance the case of the "no problem" theorists.

4 The "no-problem" camp consists primarily of Poznansky and his supporters (especially Richard Taruskin and Simon Karlinsky).

5 According to Poznansky, post -1878 "the earlier and specifically 'homosexual anxiety' ceased to be a feature of his inner life." Elsewhere, the same biographer asserts that "Tchaikovsky never exhibited any moral remorse in regard to his homosexual pursuits" (see *Tchaikovsky's Last Days*, p. 20).

6 Holden, *Tchaikovsky*, p. 271.

7 Ibid., p. 235. A few of many possible quotations from this diary will suffice to illustrate the point:

> 7 May: feasted my eyes all day on Bob. How utterly ravishing he looks in his little white suit.
> 8 May: Bob walked with me in the garden, then came to my room. Ah, what a delight this Bob is.
> 9 May: Sat in the window and chatted with [Nata and] Bob . . . Ah, what a perfect being this Bob is!
> 10 May: A stroll with Bob . . . What a little darling he is!
> 24 May: In the end, Bob will drive me mad with his unspeakable charms.

8 Between his biography (1991) and his latest monograph (1996), Poznansky shifts ground on the crucial point concerning whether Tchaikovsky and his nephew were lovers. In the biography, Poznansky is almost prudishly unprepared to consider the possibility that Tchaikovsky might have had an intimate physical relationship with his nephew, calling attention to Tchaikovsky's "unrequited" love for Bob and imputing the tragic tenor of the Sixth Symphony dedicated to him to this *lack* of fulfillment: "But it is to Bob Davidov that the Sixth Symphony is dedicated. Arguably, it was only now that the aging composer recognized the full extent of his longing for Bob, even as he faced the unlikelihood of its physical fulfillment. Tchaikovsky's letters and diaries leave no doubt that not only did he adore Bob but he also felt for him a homoerotic passion as strong as any of which he was capable. In the Sixth Symphony, dedicated to Bob, Tchaikovsky embodied the anguish of unrequited love, a conflict between platonic passion and the desires of the flesh, held forcibly in check so as not to profane the sublimity of passion" (*The Quest for the Inner Man*, pp. 558–59). In *Tchaikovsky's Last Days*, however, Poznansky leaves open the possibility that Tchaikovsky and Bob were, in fact, lovers, asserting that "There is every reason to think that by the end of 1893 Tchaikovsky's love life had assumed forms which were more than satisfactory. His relations with Bob Davidov were at an exceptionally high level, regardless of whether or not sexual intimacy was involved" (p. 22).

9 Additionally, it should be pointed out that, in every way – with the exception of his homosexuality – Tchaikovsky was a profoundly conservative if not reactionary man, particularly in his later years. Certainly his Pan-Slavic and imperialist political views and strong support for the Tsar hardly make him a proto-revolutionary (as some Soviet musicologists later tried to portray him). Perhaps, because he was loyal to the Russian Orthodox faith, he was troubled by the "sinful" nature of his relationship with Bob when considered from a strictly religious perspective; I shall attempt to show that eschatological anxieties do indeed inform the later symphonies – especially the Sixth.

10 As Susan McClary has observed, the idea of gendering thematic areas of sonata form was an article of faith for nineteenth- and twentieth-century composers. Where I believe McClary has erred is *not* in her assertion that elements of Tchaikovsky's sonata forms conform to this gendering paradigm, but rather in under-stressing the *homosexual* dimension of Tchaikovsky's gendered thematic polarities: for Tchaikovsky, the typically "feminine" second thematic group is associated with the *boy* Other.

11 Von Meck recognized that Tchaikovsky was "abnormal" and accepted him as such.

12 See Orlova, *Tchaikovsky: A Self-Portrait*, pp. 108–09; Brown, *Tchaikovsky*, vol. III, pp. 164–65.

13 Poznansky, *Tchaikovsky's Last Days*, p. 21. But Tchaikovsky's ambivalent feelings about his sexual encounters with boy prostitutes are revealed by the continuation: "I woke with remorse and full understanding of the fraudulence and exaggerated quality of that happiness which I felt yesterday and which, in substance, is nothing but a strong sexual inclination based on the correspondence with the capricious demands of my taste and on the general charm of that youth . . . And instead of helping him to better himself, I only contributed to his further going down."

14 No. 8 in *Iolanta* (*Romance de Vaudémont*).

15 This descending scale motive reappears in many different guises throughout the symphony. Several notable instances beginning on F♯ (as in the second group) include: first movement, mm. 284ff. (violins); second movement, the B section, mm. 57ff. (violins); and the Finale, bassoons, mm. 21ff. (extended *ad infernum*).

16 Brown, *Tchaikovsky*, vol. III, p. 18. Serious reading of Scripture is an interest that Tchaikovsky shared with a number of contemporary late nineteenth-century composers, most notably Brahms and Bruckner.

17 Most notably the *Liturgy of St. John Chrysostom*, Op. 41 (1878), *Nine Sacred Pieces* (1884–85), the *Hymn in Honour of SS Cyril and Theodius* (1885), and "An Angel Weeping" (1887).

18 Quoted from Christoph Rueger, program notes to *Tchaikovsky, Liturgy of St.*

John Chrysostom, Melodiya/ BMG, 1995. Orlova (*Tchaikovsky: A Self-Portrait*, pp. 84–85) provides a slightly different translation of the same passages.

19 Rueger, program notes.

20 Leviticus 18:22 plainly declares: "Thou shalt not lie with mankind, as with womankind: it is an abomination." Leviticus 20:13 continues: "If there is a man who lies with a male as those be with a woman, both of them have committed a detestable act." The New Testament also accuses the people of Sodom (the city destroyed by God because of its sexual perversity) of "a depraved passion:" "their women exchanged the natural function for that which is unnatural, and in the same way the men abandoned the natural function of women and burned in their desire towards one another, men with men, committing indecent acts" (Romans 1:24). Perhaps, most significantly for the program of the Sixth Symphony, this "evil" is to be severely punished at the Last Judgment: "Do you not know that the unrighteous will not inherit the kingdom of God? Do not be deceived; neither the immoral, nor idolaters, nor adulterers, *nor homosexuals* [my emphasis], nor thieves, nor the greedy, nor drunkards, nor revilers, nor robbers will inherit the kingdom of God" (1 Corinthians 6:9–10). 1 Timothy 1: 8–10 continues: "[Know] that the law is not made for a righteous man, but for . . . them that defile themselves with mankind . . ."

21 No. 11 in *Iolanta (Finale)*.

22 The poet Apukhtin had been Tchaikovsky's fellow student at the School of Jurisprudence and was, like Tchaikovsky, a homosexual. Tchaikovsky set a number of Apukhtin's verses and the two men enjoyed a lasting if sporadic friendship.

23 Holden, *Tchaikovsky*, p. 346; Poznansky, *Tchaikovsky's Last Days*, p. 28.

24 That the Sixth Symphony is programmatically connected with the liturgy is confirmed by the quotation of a phrase from the Russian Orthodox Requiem (in mm. 202–05 of the first movement, mentioned in Chapter 2): "With thy saints, O Christ, give peace to the soul of thy servant."

25 In his famous elucidation of the program of the Fourth Symphony, Tchaikovsky describes the beginning of this symphony with its sustained trumpet call as representing "Fate"; however, this trumpet call also has eschatological connotations, which will be discussed in greater detail later in this chapter.

26 Notice that this chord (A–C–E♭–G) is the identical sonority to the "*Tristan*" chord and the "*Pathétique*" chord at the beginning of the Finale.

27 Perhaps Tchaikovsky had this part of the *Pathétique* in mind when he wrote to Bob, "I am suffering not only from an anguish beyond mere words (in my new symphony there is a passage that seems to me to express it well) . . ." (quoted from Holden, *Tchaikovsky*, p. 336).

28 Brown, *Tchaikovsky*, vol. IV, 406.

29 Klaus Theweleit asks "What then constitutes the particular attraction of homosexuality to the fascist male?": "My suspicion is that it is its capacity to be associated with power and transgression. Homosexual practice is one of the few remaining gaps through which he [i.e. the fascist male] can escape the compulsory encoding of feared heterosexuality; it is an escape from normality, from a whole domain of more or less permissible pleasures – all encoded with 'femininity.' As a homosexual, the fascist can prove, both to himself and others, that he is 'non-bourgeois,' and boldly defiant of normality" (*Male Fantasies*, vol. II, *Male Bodies: Psychoanalyzing the White Terror*, trans. Erica Carter and Chris Turner [Minneapolis: University of Minnesota Press, 1989], p. 322).

30 Volkov, *A Cultural History of St. Petersburg*, p. 113.

31 Brown, *Tchaikovsky*, vol. IV, p. 339.

32 In the story of the Pied Piper, the rats symbolize the Jews; the moral of the story is that once one unleashes genocide, who knows where it will stop (the good townsfolk realize – too late – that their own children are next in line to be exterminated). Nazis played on this equation of Jews with rats. For example, in the Nazi propaganda film *Jud Süss* (1940), the Jews are associated with "large groups" of rats. Zyklon B, the gas used in the gas chambers, was, in fact, related to a product developed to exterminate vermin in homes and apartments.

33 George L. Mosse, *Toward the Final Solution. A History of European Racism* (Madison: University of Wisconsin Press, 1985), p. 220.

34 Greenberg, *The Construction of Homosexuality*, p. 107, "Sparta, too, institutionalized homosexual relations between mature men and adolescent boys, as well as between adult women and girls, and gave them a pedagogical focus."

35 In the Renaissance, Dürer's self-identification with the Messiah was not considered blasphemy; rather, it was regarded as an act of homage: by participating in Christ's suffering, the artist also partook of the redemption effected by His ultimate sacrifice.

36 The Cross-motives in *Romeo and Juliet* and the Sixth Symphony activate two distinct but related iconographic traditions: firstly, "Christ on the Cross," and secondly, "*Ecce homo*," i.e. Christ paraded before the people after his religious and civil trials, the last stage of the Passion before the Crucifixion. The iconography of *Ecce homo* derives from John 19:4–7, where Christ is described as mocked by the Romans as "King of the Jews," crowned with thorns and made to hold a reed scepter in his bound hands. In this pitiable condition, he is exhibited to the contemptuous horde.

37 In the preceding discussion, I characterized the descending-scale motive as the "Bob"-motive and the associated music in D major (in all movements of the symphony) with Bob as "the beloved." How appropriate it is, then, that

Tchaikovsky's "longing" as a lover should be represented by the sequentially *ascending*, "ardent" "yearning" motive, while the beloved Bob is characterized by the much smoother, more poised *descending* scalar motives.

38 I do not mean to suggest that *every* instance of this configuration signifies the "Cross" in tonal music; rather, this *topos* is activated here by the particular combination of contextual factors. A clear example of the Cross-motive is provided by Pergolesi at the opening of his *Stabat Mater*, and one could cite many further examples of the Cross-motive from the late Baroque in Vivaldi, Lotti, Bach, and Handel. That the Cross-motive continued to be an important *topos* in nineteenth-century musical rhetoric is demonstrated by the "cathedral" movement of Schumann's Third "Rhenish" Symphony. Tchaikovsky's cruciform symbolism is taken up by later Russian composers, including Shostakovich and Schnittke. For a discussion of the Cross-motive in Shostakovich, where the composer employs it to represent himself as a crucified "Jewish" Christ, see Timothy L. Jackson, "Dmitry Shostakovich: The Composer as Jew," in *Shostakovich Reconsidered*, ed. Allan Ho and Dmitri Feofanov (London: Toccata Press, 1998), 567–609.

39 The inspiration for this famous melody (as noted earlier) was probably Tchaikovsky's fifteen-year old Conservatory pupil Eduard Zak, with whom the composer was passionately in love at the time.

40 Observe that this theme also embodies the "cruciform" tetrachords G–A♭–C–D♭ and D–E♭–B♭–A♭.

41 Laurence's new chorale-like theme contains the tetrachord A–B–D–C♯, a traditional contrapuntal *topos* with connotations of the Crucifixion. Such cruciform allusions were absent from Laurence's original genial, lyrical theme in the first version, which came in for some harsh criticism from Balakirev (who had provided the impetus for the work's composition); he complained to Tchaikovsky:

> The first [Friar's] theme is not at all to my taste. Perhaps when it's worked out it achieves some degree of beauty, but when written out unadorned in the way you've sent it to me, it conveys neither beauty nor strength, and doesn't even depict the character of Friar Laurence in the way required. Here there ought to be something like Liszt's chorales (*Der nächtliche Zug* in F sharp, *Hunnen-schlacht* and "St Elizabeth") with an ancient Catholic character resembling that of Orthodox [church music]. But instead your E major tune has a completely different character – the character of quartet themes by Haydn, that genius of petty-bourgeois music, who arouses a strong thirst for beer. (Quoted from Brown, *Tchaikovsky*, vol. I, pp. 182–83.)

Taking Balakirev's critique to heart, in place of the Friar's amiable E major melody, which opens the first version, Tchaikovsky substituted the somber, chorale-like melody with its cruciform tetrachord (second version, mm.

1–11). Of particular interest is the appearance of the Baroque *topos* of the "Cross" slightly later in the introduction in the interlocking ("crossing") flute and clarinet parts (mm. 21–27). By activating this traditional, sacred topic of the Cross, Tchaikovsky succeeded in evoking the "ancient Catholic character" that Balakirev had prescribed. But he achieved much more than that. And by invoking the Cross-motive, the introduction does more than simply portray Laurence: it foreshadows and foreordains his role in the "crucifixion" of the lovers, i.e. he executes divine "justice" upon them as punishment for their "forbidden" love.

42 The new Cross-motive is in mm. 21ff. in the flutes and clarinets, the individual lines crossing as the flute states the cruciform tetrachord F–E♭–A♭–G♭. To underscore the allusion to the lovers' sacrificial "crucifixion," the passage evokes the opening of the *Stabat Mater* of Pergolesi.

43 If we return, momentarily, to the first (1869) version of the development, Tchaikovsky derives its material almost exclusively from the "fight" and "love/Juliet" themes. As Brown has observed, there is a felicitous relationship between the first "fight" theme with its falling fifth F♯–B and its rising third B–C♯–D, the "new" "fight" theme in the first version of the development (mm. 257–58), and the "Juliet" theme's incipit. But conspicuously absent from the main body of the development is the original Friar Laurence theme, which appears only once at the development's climax over the prolonged dominant (mm. 295–304, flutes and trumpets). By contrast, the revised development concentrates on Friar Laurence's new theme from the revised introduction.

44 If the introduction and exposition present the cast of characters (the Friar, and the rival Montagues and Capulets) and the initial action (Romeo's initial meeting with Juliet and their overwhelming love), the development initiates the "working out" of the plot, i.e. the main body of the action. The emphasis on the Friar Laurence chorale in the second version of the development embodies Tchaikovsky's reinterpretation of the play whereby Laurence – as the instrument of Divine retribution – becomes the prime mover (in the first version, the single appearance of his theme at the end of the development seemed incidental and unmotivated). The great weight that Tchaikovsky now places on the Friar's role can be justified in Shakespeare's play: it is Laurence who propels the action: it is he who marries Romeo and Juliet without advising their families, devises Juliet's fake death but then fails to properly report the ruse to Romeo, and, instead of staying with Juliet to comfort her when she awakens next to her dead lover, deserts her. In Shakespeare, abandoned by this fickle representative of religion, and perhaps by God Himself, Juliet commits suicide. But in Tchaikovsky's revision of the overture, the Friar is reinterpreted not as Shakespeare's genial yet cowardly

creature but as the harsh, all-seeing, unforgiving Angel of Death who deliberately abandons Juliet to her fate. Screamed forth by the trumpets (mm. 235–343), the Friar's theme now echoes the Last Trump.

This Last Judgment eschatology at the climax of the development is reactivated in the recapitulation by the second version of the *dénouement* (1870: mm. 419ff.). In the first version of the plot's climax (1869: mm. 390–406), Tchaikovsky too simplistically represents the general collapse with a descending bass line highlighted by its oblique relationship to whirling pedal-ostinati in the upper voice. In the much more sophisticated 1870 reading, Tchaikovsky continues the "love/Juliet–Zak" music (mm. 419ff.), its tonally "drifting" harmonies – i.e. Schoenberg's "vagrant" harmonies – representing the progressive "derailment" of the Friar's plan. Then, when the Friar's theme reasserts itself in mm. 450–53 and mm. 458–61 – the trumpets now supported by full brass, oboe, and cor anglais – it assumes its most terrible aspect as a "Call to Judgement." The final, 1880 revision affecting the end of the recapitulation and coda (mm. 461ff.) achieves, as Brown aptly observes, "a melodic fusing which signifies the ultimate catastrophe as elements of the conflict music infiltrate destructively into the broad love theme, [and] swiftly overwhelm it" (Brown, *Tchaikovsky*, vol. I, p. 194).

45 In the March, as in *Tristan*, the lovers "meet" at the point when the structural dominant is achieved (here, D as V of G major in m. 221).

46 See especially the quote from George Mosse, *The Creation of Modern Masculinity* (Oxford: Oxford University Press, 1996), and the surrounding discussion on pp. 3–12 above.

47 Notice that *Manfred's* most striking Tristanisms, which are generically related to those of the *Pathétique's Adagio lamentoso*, include: the emphasis on the sonority of the half-diminished seventh chord to represent Manfred's tortured personality (i.e. the "*Tristan* chord" = the "*Manfred*" chord = the "*Pathétique*" chord), and the use of the *Tristan* auxiliary cadence model in the first movement of *Manfred*.

48 Poundie Burstein, "A New View of *Tristan*: Tonal Unity in the *Prelude* and Conclusion to Act 1," *Theory and Practice* 8 (1983), 15–41. The initial note A, and the strong suggestion of the A minor tonality, are not simply to be "read away"; rather, the suggestion of A minor (and later A major) is a very important aspect of the *Prelude*. But, when considered in the larger context of the C-rooted tonality of the first act (and the opera as a whole), the initial implied A minor chord can be understood to displace a C chord, A displacing the G of the C chord as in a 6–5 exchange (the other two tones C and E being held in common). This compositional idea of A or A♭ (C major: VI or ♭VI) displacing G as the understood fifth of the C chord proves to be very important throughout the opera. For example, in Act 1,

mm. 227–28, as Isolde approaches her vocal cadence on C, the bass articulates A♭, which displaces the G in the C chord (here, as elsewhere, the A♭–G displacement is associated with the effect of a deceptive cadence). Similarly, within the so-called *Todes-Motiv* (first articulated in mm. 318ff.), the A♭ of the first chord (m. 318) displaces an understood G, which is provided only when the bass descends chromatically to the G in m. 324. Many examples of this kind of displacement of C by A or A♭ chords could be cited. One particularly striking passage, which occurs near the end of Act 1 just before the *Prelude* is recomposed, mm. 1821ff. (i.e. just after Brangäne's outcry "volles Werk blüht jammernd empor"), may serve as a representative example. In mm. 1818–21 the music sounds as if it will cadence strongly on the tonic C, but the C chord is displaced by a first inversion A♭ chord as G is displaced by A♭. As a result of this displacement, on a deeper structural level, the arrival of the tonic is delayed until the very end of the act.

49 In Act 1, the bass reiterates the E–G–C auxiliary cadence as follows: E (m. 1)–G (m. 104) – C (m. 167), (1) E (m. 840)–G (m. 860) – C (understood, m. 862), (2) E (m. 1038 = Prelude) – G (m. 1049) – C (m. 1051), (3) E (m. 1159) – G (m. 1167) – C (m. 1168), (4) E (m. 1265 = Prelude) – G (m. 1276) – C (m. 1286), (5) E (m. 1560 = Prelude) – G (m. 1609) – C (m. 1611), (6) E (m. 1760 = Prelude) – G (m. 1876) – G (m. 1906), (8) E (m. 1914) – G (m. 1921), (9) E (m. 1926) – G (m.1940) – C (m. 1946).

50 However, if we posit the expected B in m. 1631, we recognize that the second scene (mm. 998–1631) is controlled by a chromatic deformation of the "yearning" cadence: III (E, m. 998) moving to ♭V = ♯IV (G♭ = F♯, m. 1473) to cadence on the expected ♭I = VII (C♭ = B, m. 1631).

51 Notice that Wagner embeds yet another recomposition of the III–V–I paradigm within the prolongation of F minor spanning mm. 1–634 as E (m. 441) – G (m. 472) – C (m. 584), C functioning in context as the dominant of F.

52 Wagner (as Tchaikovsky rightly observed) employs symphonic structures in opera; but Tchaikovsky is no less "guilty" of transposing the harmonic symbolism of opera into the symphony and song-cycle.

53 Furthermore, these instances of harmonic arrival are also the junctures in the narrative when – again, as in *Tristan* – the central characters are condemned to death. In the *Pathétique*, the crucial points where the music attains the structural dominant are: in the first movement mm. 267ff., in the March mm. 221ff., and in the Finale mm. 126ff. But whereas, for Wagner, "love-death" proves redemptive, in Tchaikovsky's critical *Tristan*-deformations, death becomes simply "descent into nothingness."

54 Additionally, Karlinsky ("Should We Retire Tchaikovsky?" pp. 20–21) calls attention to an important yet subtle motivic connection between this passage

and the second group in the exposition, namely that the descending-scale Bob-motive reappears in the flutes and violins (mm. 284–300).

55 As Brown has observed, this music is closely related to the passage depicting the Voyevoda's death in the coda of the *Voyevoda* Symphonic Ballad (mm. 460–end). In the Ballad (1891), an elderly general discovers his young wife with her lover and orders his servant to shoot the wife while he murders the youth. But the servant disobeys and, turning his gun on the general, kills him instead of the wife. In both the *Voyevoda* and the Sixth Symphony, Tchaikovsky draws upon various musical conventions to represent Destiny severing the thread of life. And in both the *Voyevoda* Ballad and the Sixth Symphony, the Oracle intones the "stabbing" death sentence through the "voice" of the lower brass. In the *Pathétique*, the overall descent of the "Bob-motive" in the upper strings (from the high f$\sharp^2$ in m. 284 to the low b in m. 299) foreshadows the ultimate collapse (in the Finale), the string chorus imitating the brass, resonating with it in a manner reminiscent of an ancient Greek chorus echoing Fate's stern and irreversible decree. When Bob's "youth" music returns in the reprise of the second group (mm. 305–34), it does so in the key of B major. But after the Oracle's terrifying death sentence, Bob's music now has an entirely different effect. In the exposition, in D major, it was genuinely warm, seductive, and, as noted earlier, idyllic; but here in the recapitulation, in B major, its effect is chilling. This is the "transfigured" B major with which *Tristan's Liebestod* concludes: the ice-cold peace of the lovers' embrace in death.

56 Quoted from Barbara Eschenberg, *Der Kampf der Geschlechter. Der neue Mythos in der Kunst 1850–1930* (Munich: Lenbachhaus, 1995), p. 252.

57 The F–B tritonality of the Fourth Symphony has programmatic-metaphorical significance, the underlying harmonic "abnormality" representing homosexual "deviance from a norm"; as such, it becomes emblematic for Tchaikovsky's "homosexual problem" in all its complexity. Since Tchaikovsky links the "devilish" tritonal progression I–$\sharp$IV/$\flat$V with his "anomaly," I have referred to the composer's tritonal background harmonic progressions as his "homosexual tritonality." I would submit that McClary has drawn a valid – and important – parallel between the tritonal "seduction" of Don José by his fantasy of Carmen, and the homosexual, tritonal "entrapment" of the protagonist of the Fourth Symphony, "ensnared" by his "dream boy" (see McClary, *Feminine Endings*, pp. 59–65).

58 These large-scale sequences are composed of minor thirds (e.g. first movement of the Fourth Symphony: F–A$\flat$–C$\flat$/B–D) and major thirds (third movement of the Fourth Symphony: F–A–D$\flat$–F), as well as the more common sequences of perfect fourths and fifths.

59 See Jackson, "Sexuality and Structure in Tchaikovsky," exx. 1b–c.

60 Tchaikovsky received the vocal score of *Carmen* in March 1875 from Vladi-

mir Shilovsky, who had been profoundly impressed by the opera's very first performance on 3 March 1875. On 20 January 1876, Tchaikovsky saw *Carmen* staged for the first time; Modest noted the importance of the event for Pyotr Ilyitch noting that "Rarely have I seen my brother so deeply moved by a performance in the theatre." The Fourth Symphony was conceived at the beginning of 1877, i.e. precisely in the period after Tchaikovsky had "discovered" *Carmen*. Tchaikovsky described the opera as "a masterpiece," and was especially moved by the final scene. Apparently, it hit him with the full force of a revelation; and his fascination with it would last to the end of his life. He is reported to have studied the score on numerous occasions, subjecting it to the most careful and thorough-going analysis. I am proposing that Tchaikovsky not only studied *Carmen*; he achieved full maturity as a composer by *re-forming* – that is, by recreating – essential aspects of Bizet's masterpiece in his Fourth Symphony. That the F–B tritonality of the Fourth Symphony is not simply a norm of Tchaikovsky's Russian harmonic language is confirmed by comparing the tonal-formal organization of the sonata-form outer movements of the first symphonic trilogy with that of the Fourth Symphony's first movement. The background harmonic structures of the sonata forms in Symphonies Nos. 1–3 are, for the most part, conventionally diatonic; indeed, these earlier sonata forms conform fairly closely to the harmonic patterns of German sonata-form models.

61 McClary, *Feminine Endings*, pp. 59–67.

62 In *Carmen*, Act 4, Duet and Final Chorus, the bass articulates the overall motion from (F minor:) I–V–♭II as F–B–C–G♭ by dividing the tritones into minor thirds: F (Carmen: je ne t'aime plus) – A♭ (Carmen: je l'aime et devant la mort) – B (understood above E at the crowd's Viva!) and C (Don José: Ainsi le salut) – E♭ (crowd: Victoire!) – G♭ (Don José: Eh bien! Damnée).

63 F–B tritonality controls the large-scale tonal structure of the ballet as a whole: Acts 1–2, and 4 are in B minor, while Act 3 is in F major-minor; thus, the tonality of the four acts is B–F–B.

64 Beginning with the end of Act 2, the bass ascends tritonally F♯–C: F♯ (end of Act II) – D♯/E♭ (beginning of Act 3) – C (entrance of the choir). From C, the bass descends through A (Countess's ghost to Lisa's aria) back down to F♯ (Lisa's suicide at the end of the scene). Over the course of the last three scenes (in the gambling house), the bass moves from A (as mediant of F♯ in No. 22) back to C at the point when the dying Hermann is accorded a vision of Lisa in Heaven (end of No. 24). More specifically, when Hermann stabs himself as a consequence of Fate's duplicity and the ghost's final triumphant appearance, the music ascends from A to C through a subsidiary sequence of ascending fifths A–D–G–C.

65 The B♭ of the B section (mm. 60–118) is prolonged *through* the first return to F in the A′ section (mm. 119–48): the bass ascends from B♭ through D in the B′ section (mm. 149–98) and E in the introduction's interpolated reprise (mm. 199–222) to the F of the second, definitive return of the A′ section (mm. 249–end), i.e. F–B♭–D–E–F (F major: I–IV–VI–VII–I). Thus, the tritone B♭–E is "healed" by its resolution to the perfect fifth B♭–F.

66 In the Fifth Symphony (Appendix C), the "fateful" macro-symphonic ascending fifth sequence bifurcates in the second movement, the slow movement simultaneously suggesting two possible continuations. Sequence 1 (the notes placed in boxes), a sequence of ascending fifths generated from E at the end of the first movement, becomes a "dead end": E (first movement) – B–F♯ (second movement); Sequence 2 (the circled notes), on the other hand, an overlapping sequence of ascending fifths generated from the second movement's D, proves "victorious," opening up the path to the Finale: D (second movement) – A (third movement) – E (Finale). The overlap of the two macro-symphonic sequences creates the curious effect of B minor / D major bitonality in the slow movement, the definitive "victory" of D major over B minor being achieved only in the coda (mm. 170ff.).

67 In my "Sexuality and Structure in Tchaikovsky" (p. 22), I suggested that "in the elegiac last movement of the Sixth Symphony – the '*Adagio lamentoso*,' a kind of death certificate – the cause of death is graphically depicted (through *Augenmusik*) in the opening gesture. The hero . . . like the melodic line, has been 'torn apart' by his condition (the striking division of the linear progression, essentially the descending fourth F♯–E–D–C♯, between the first and second violins . . .)." The cause of death is further analyzed in the music: the protagonist's perfect fourth (F♯–E–D–C♯, D–C♯–B–A, and B–A–G–F♯: bracket "x" in Appendix A) has been "perverted" by enlargements of the "deformed" *augmented* fourth (F♯–C, bracket "y"). I call the reader's attention to a point *not* made in my article (although implicit in my earlier remarks), namely that the structural upper voice of the march (B–A–G) is, in context, part of an enlargement of "x" (Appendix A, c–d).

68 No. 6 in *Iolanta* (Scène et Monologue d'Ibn Hakia).

69 Thus, voice and piano together contribute to the linear-chromatic line a♭² (m. 31) – b♭♭² (mm. 32–33) – b♭ (m. 34).

5 Compositional genesis: the Six Romances Op. 73 and the *Pathétique*

1 The sketchbook has been published in facsimile (see bibliography).

2 As the senior archivist at the Tchaikovsky House Museum in Klin, Paulina Vaidman, has proposed; see "Unbekannter Čajkovskij," pp. 281–91 (I shall

return to this question). Vaidman provides Kohlhase's transcription of the draft for the "Concert Piece."

3 Supporting Vaidman's hypothesis is the texture of the draft, which, in mm. 1–30 and 45–60, consistently presents the solo 'cello(?) line in the upper staff of the three-system layout. However, even if this is a draft for the projected "Concert Piece" rather than the *Pathétique*, the music appears to be connected with the Finale of the Sixth Symphony. Firstly, the draft is in B minor, the main key of the symphony. Secondly, the strong insistence on the Neapolitan C major chord (mm. 24–31) parallels the same emphasis in the final version of the Finale (especially mm. 75–81). This emphasis on the Neapolitan in both the draft and the *Adagio lamentoso* gives this music a tragic character in keeping with the overall tone of the *Pathétique*. A third correspondence is metrical: the 9/8 alternating with 3/4 meter of the sketch is clearly the same as the 9/8 alternating with 3/4 meter of the B section of the Finale as notated in the sketches on pp. 50–51. Finally, the melancholy descending ninth in the "'cello" part (mm. 5–8), which "droops" listlessly from d^2 to $c\sharp^1$, resembles the descent in the bassoons in mm. 12–18 of the Finale. Thus, if this draft was intended for a separate "Concert Piece" rather than the Finale of the Sixth Symphony, nevertheless it does seem to be generically related to the Sixth Symphony.

4 See Brown, *Tchaikovsky*, Vol. IV, p. 463.

6 Deconstructing homosexual *grande passion pathétique*

1 Quoted from Poznansky, *Tchaikovsky's Last Days*, p. 57.

2 *Tchaikovsky's Last Days*, p. 57.

3 As Helene Berg would later explain the true nature of her husband's relationship with Hanna Fuchs-Robettin to Alma Mahler shortly after Berg's death: "He himself constructed obstacles and thereby created the romanticism he required . . . In *this* way and *only* in this way could the *Lyric Suite* [1926] have come to be." Quoted from George Perle, *The Operas of Alban Berg. Lulu* (Berkeley: University of California Press, 1985), pp. 28–29.

4 Kraus, "The 'Russian' Influence in the First Symphony of Jean Sibelius," p. 142.

5 John Warrack, program note for Sibelius, Symphony No. 1, conducted by Herbert von Karajan, EMI (1987) CDM 7 69028 2.

6 The fact that this is an early comment is significant because later in life Sibelius generally told people whatever they wanted to hear. But Sibelius had no reason to dissimulate in a private letter to Aino.

7 The conductor of the orchestra in which the young Sibelius played, Richard Faltin, had come from Danzig (then in West Prussia); his first and most infl-

uential composition teacher, Martin Wegelius, was educated in Leipzig and Munich. He studied music theory from Lobe's *Lehrbuch der musikalischen Composition*. In his manuscripts, Sibelius writes and thinks in German and Swedish. If influence is to be discerned, that of Goldmark (for a short period his teacher in Vienna), Wagner, Liszt, but especially Bruckner (whose music he had heard and greatly admired in Vienna) is clear. The typically Sibelian notion of gradual "crystallization," as he put it, owes much to Bruckner, whose music also tends to develop slowly and inexorably toward distant goals. One could argue that certain features of Bruckner's Third, Fourth, and Seventh Symphonies, as published in their first editions (1885, 1889–90), and Brahms's Fourth Symphony (1884) influenced Sibelius profoundly. Sibelius's 1894 tone poem *Skogsraet*, which concludes with a tragic Adagio, might appear to be indebted to the *Pathétique*, but this possibility can be dismissed on both chronological and genetic grounds: the work began as an aborted opera based on a libretto fashioned during Sibelius's sojourn in Bayreuth and Munich (in August 1894); composition of *Skogsraet* was well under way before the first Finnish performance of the *Pathétique*.

8 Bearing in mind Sibelius's Germanic musical roots, my own view is that his First Symphony, with its tragic conclusion in E minor, may be more indebted to Brahms's Fourth Symphony than to any Russian symphony.

9 For a discussion of large-scale auxiliary cadences in Sibelius, see Jackson, "'A Heart of Ice': Crystallization in Sibelius's *Pohjola's Daughter* and Other Works."

10 Rakhmaninov was exposed to Tchaikovsky's music from a very early point in his career. He was introduced to Tchaikovsky personally when he was twelve years old; by thirteen, he had already made a four-hand piano arrangement of the *Manfred* Symphony (in 1886). For his part, Tchaikovsky was deeply impressed with Rakhmaninov as a young composer and pianist. At the premiere of Rakhmaninov's graduation "exercise," the opera *Aleko*, Tchaikovsky clapped ostentatiously. He awarded the young composer-pianist the unprecedented grade of "5++" on his final examination at the Moscow Conservatory, and recommended his music for publication. Tchaikovsky's sudden death deprived Rakhmaninov of an influential mentor and patron. The young composer mourned Tchaikovsky in his Elegiac Trio No. 2 in D minor Op. 9, a work clearly modeled on Tchaikovsky's Trio in A minor Op. 50, and (like the Tchaikovsky) dedicated "to the memory of a great artist." Rakhmaninov still felt indebted to Tchaikovsky much later in his career. In the manuscript of the fourth movement of the *Bells* (composed in 1913) at the words "and we weep, and remember," Rakhmaninov wrote "P[yotr] Tchaik[ovsky]."

11 Like the symphony's failure, the termination of the affair must have been a

tremendous blow, contributing to Rakhmaninov's three-year compositional silence (c. 1897–1900).

12 Bertensson and Leyda, *Sergei Rachmaninoff. A Lifetime in Music*, p. 60.

13 Ibid.

14 The title *The Crag* refers to a poem by Lermontov. Rakhmaninov inscribed the manuscript with the poem's opening lines: "A little golden cloud slept the night / on the breast of a giant crag." This couplet simultaneously connects the music programmatically to Chekhov's story "On the Road" (1885), where these lines are also cited as an epigram for the ensuing action. Both the Chekhov story and the Rakhmaninov tone poem describe the hopeless love of a lonely and disillusioned man for a beautiful, sensitive young woman whom he meets by chance in a deserted inn on Christmas eve. The next day, the man sadly witnesses the departure of her sleigh; standing in the storm, immobilized and covered with snow, he metamorphoses into a crag. Rakhmaninov's tragic music seems to embody not only the man's unrequited longing for the young woman but the composer's own yearning for Anna.

15 This biographical detail is a further indication that Tchaikovsky did not plan to commit suicide.

16 The D of the First Symphony is also the tonal goal of the Symphonic Dances, this tonal connection being reinforced by explicit motivic references to the First Symphony in the Dances. Symphonies Nos. 2–3 move through descending fifths from E (No. 2) through A (No. 3) to D (Symphonic Dances), while the Dances themselves reinforce the culminating cadence on D by means of an auxiliary cadence of ascending fifths moving from C (First Dance) through G (Second Dance) to D (Third Dance).

17 Maria Biesold, *Rachmaninoff. Zwischen Moskau und New York, Eine Künstlerbiographie* (Berlin: Quadriga, 1993), p. 102 reports that Anna Lodizhenskaya forbade Rakhmaninov to visit her shortly after the premiere of the First Symphony. It was to Dr. Nicolai Dahl, who had helped him to recover from debilitating depression, that the Second Piano Concerto (sketched in 1900 and completed in 1901) was dedicated.

18 Rakhmaninov's "inversion" of Tchaikovsky's discourse can be seen *in nuce* in his use of Russian Orthodox *znamenny* chant-like melodies. If Tchaikovsky's quotation of the *Dies irae* in *Manfred* and the Russian Requiem in the first movement of the *Pathétique* – these chant quotations seem to have profoundly impressed Rakhmaninov – represents implacable divine judgement, for Rakhmaninov, already beginning with the First Symphony, chant-like melodies assume a personal significance which, in the post-1900 music, becomes connected with the "healing" process. The passionate chant-like melody in the Finale of the First Symphony (mm. 47ff.) intimates the "Passion" of the composer as tortured and ultimately doomed lover. But in

the Third Symphony (1936), the chant-like motto which appears at the beginning, perhaps representing "faith" and "perseverance," in the Finale does battle with and eventually triumphs over the *Dies irae*, which evokes "death" and "entropy." This "healing" implication of the chant is pursued in the Symphonic Dances (1940) where it finds its apotheosis in the final dance. Here, the "little" *znamenny* chant, which had formed the basis for the ninth, "resurrection" movement of the Vespers, intimates personal resurrection, thereby signifying spiritual "healing" and "rebirth" even as the body fails.

19 In Rakhmaninov's First Symphony (as in Tchaikovsky's Fourth Symphony), implacable Destiny, as the agent of divine "vengeance" (here punishment for the sin of adultery), is represented by a recurring opening motto (the "snap" figure).

20 Perhaps Anna intuited Rakhmaninov's program and rightly took offense at his misogynistic "murder" of his beloved by compelling her – at least in the symphonic narrative – to commit suicide.

21 As in the First Symphony, the symphonic narrative seems to have a personal, autobiographical significance. At the turn of the century, Rakhmaninov had fallen in love with his first cousin Natalya Satina and, embarking on a new liaison "forbidden" by the Russian Orthodox Church, he sought to marry her. Finally, in 1902, a priest was found who would agree to perform the marriage, and the ceremony was conducted "under wraps" in an army barracks on the edge of Moscow – to the amazement of the soldiers.

22 Martyn, *Rachmaninoff*, p. 183 designates this motive in the opera "the money-lender" and also notes its re-appearance in the Second Symphony, without commenting on its significance for the *symphonic* narrative.

23 The crisis is reached in the third movement, where the "forbidden" love-dialogue, which is clearly identified with the love-duet between Paolo and Francesca in the Second Tableau of *Francesca da Rimini*, is interrupted by anxious statements of the Salomon-motive (Rehearsal 48 + 4); but the rest of the movement gradually "assimilates" the Salomon-motive within the love music.

24 Martyn, *Rachmaninoff*, p. 340.

25 The discourse concerning Alma begins with the Adagietto in the Fifth Symphony and continues through to the end of the Tenth Symphony. However, in the following discussion I shall focus on the narratives in the Sixth, Ninth, and Tenth Symphonies within that larger discourse.

26 Brown, *Tchaikovsky*, vol. IV, p. 385.

27 Constantin Floros, *Gustav Mahler. The Symphonies*, trans. Vernon Wicker (Portland: Amadeus Press, 1993), p. 276.

28 Henry-Louis de La Grange, *Gustav Mahler*, vol I. *Vienna: The Years of Challenge* (Oxford: Oxford University Press, 1995), p. 339.

29 La Grange, *Gustav Mahler,* vol. IV, p. 635.

30 Zoltan Roman, *Gustav Mahler's American Years 1907–1911. A Documentary History* (Stuyvesant, NY: Pendragon Press, 1989), p. 447.

31 La Grange, *Gustav Mahler,* vol. IV, p. 635.

32 See Wolfgang Gratzer, *Zur "wunderlichen Mystik" Alban Bergs* (Vienna: Böhlau, 1993), pp. 93–100.

33 Floros, *Gustav Mahler. The Symphonies,* p. 191. The statements attributed to Mahler are quoted in a letter from Alphons Diepenbrock to his friend Johanna Jongkindt of 17 October 1909: "There are also typically Jewish things (You know that I am a Jew!) such as the trombone solos *Wir gehn nach Lindenau, dort ist der Himmel blau!*"

34 Peter Franklin, *The Life of Mahler* (Cambridge: Cambridge University Press, 1997), p. 197.

35 In the first movement, the I–VI–IV–V–I paradigm is realized as follows: I (A, first group) through VI (F, second group, mm. 77ff.) to IV (D, in the development, mm. 183ff., prolonged through the reprise of both the first and second groups) to V (E, mm. 395ff.) to I (A, in the coda, mm. 449ff.). In the Finale, this harmonic model is recomposed: I (A, first group, mm. 114ff.) to IV (D, the second group, mm. 191ff. prolonged through the development and both the reprise of introduction and second group, mm. 520ff.) to V (E, mm. 612ff.) to I (A, recapitulation of the first group, mm. 642ff.).

36 It is significant that, in both his Ninth and Tenth Symphonies, Mahler caricatures himself as a "Jewish" Christ – rather than the "Aryan" Christ of Wagner and the German nationalist Christian movement – with "limping" rhythmic motives. In his 1921 study of *Die Juden in der Karikatur,* Eduard Fuchs observes that (in addition to their beards and hooked noses), Jews can be identified by their demonic, "awkward" gait, i.e. as flat-footed and bow-legged (because of their generic affinity with the cloven-hoofed Devil). In a passage on Jewish painters in *Der Mythus des 20. Jahrhunderts,* Alfred Rosenberg criticizes the painter Schwalbach for having (like Mahler) put the Jew back in Christ by stigmatizing the Messiah with the typically "Jewish" features of flat-footedness and bow-leggedness.

37 For a detailed discussion of Michelangelo's youthful Virgins, see Leo Steinberg, "The Metaphors of Love and Birth in Michelangelo's *Pietàs,*" in *Studies in Erotic Art,* ed. Theodore Bowie and Cornelia V. Christenson (New York: Basic Books, 1970), pp. 231–338.

38 Floros, *Mahler,* p. 299. Mahler consulted Freud on 26 August 1910.

39 Quoted from Steinberg, "Love and Birth," p. 239.

40 Albrecht von Massow (*Halbwelt, Kultur und Natur in Alban Bergs Lulu* [Stuttgart: Franz Steiner Verlag, 1992], p. 195) calls attention to the appearance of the "*Tristan*" chord at this climactic point in the opera.

41 Roy Travis, "The Recurrent Figure in the Britten/Piper Opera *Death in Venice*," in *The Music Forum*, vol. IV, part I, ed. Felix Salzer and Carl Schachter (New York: Columbia University Press, 1987), pp. 129–246.

42 Elizabeth Wilson, *Shostakovich. A Life Remembered* (Princeton: Princeton University Press, 1994), p. 340.

43 Ibid.

44 Like Mahler, Shostakovich puts himself as "the Jew" back in Christ; see Timothy L. Jackson, "Dmitry Shostakovich: The Composer as Jew," in *Shostakovich Reconsidered*, ed. Allan Ho and Dmitri Feofanov (London: Toccata Press, 1998), pp. 567–609.

45 Solomon Volkov, *Testimony. The Memoirs of Dmitri Shostakovich* (New York: Harper and Row, 1979), pp. 140–41.

46 Ibid., p. 146.

47 Alexander Ivashkin, *Alfred Schnittke* (London: Phaidon, 1996), p. 166.

48 Edward Rothstein, *New York Times*, 2 August 1994.

49 Ronald Weitzman, program notes for Alfred Schnittke, Symphony No. 6. Symphony No. 7, conducted by Tadaaki Otaka, BIS Cd-747, 1996.

50 Bachmann, *Karajan*, p. 88.

51 Prieberg, *Kraftprobe*. The same author essentially recapitulates his position in "Furtwängler: Repräsentant oder Saboteur?" Unknown to Prieberg, Heinrich Schenker's unpublished diary contains repeated mentions of Furtwängler's anti-Semitic utterances, although in the conductor's favor, it should be noted that he consistently helped Schenker, who was Jewish. One might say that Furtwängler's anti-Semitism, like that of many cultured Germans, was genteel and highly selective.

52 Michael H. Kater, *The Twisted Muse. Musicians and Their Music in the Third Reich* (Oxford: Oxford University Press, 1997), p. 202.

53 Mengelberg recorded the *Pathétique* for Telefunken on 22 April 1941. According to information found in *Willem Mengelberg, Conductor, Exhibition Catalogue* (The Hague: Haags Gemeentemuseum, 1996), p. 151, as late as 24 and 26 February, and 25 April 1944, Mengelberg was permitted by State Commissioner Seyss-Inquart to conduct the *Pathétique*.

54 Quoted from Bachmann, *Karajan*, p. 104.

55 A comparison of Furtwängler's 1937, 1942, and 1951 performances of the March from the Ninth Symphony may serve to highlight the impact of political circumstances upon interpretation; it suggests that Furtwängler's interpretations – no less than Karajan's – are political improvisations (see Dennis, *Beethoven in German Politics*, pp. 142–176). The 1937 London performance was part of celebrations surrounding the coronation of George VI and connected with Nazi Germany's effort to improve both relations with Britain and its international image ("Alle Menschen werden Brüder" being the

watchword of the day). The 1942 Berlin performance was associated with Hitler's birthday celebrations. The 1951 concert marked the re-opening of Bayreuth. In the 1937 and 1942 versions of the fugue following the *Alla marcia*, Furtwängler unleashes an inhumanly fast tempo surpassing the capacity of the orchestral players to articulate the notes. As in Karajan's 1939 recording of the *Pathétique*'s March, it is as if the "Master Race's" aspirations for world domination are being realized in music (perhaps the 1937 English Beethoven performance also carries an implicit warning of German renewed vigor). By contrast, the post-war reading of this passage is considerably slower, much more subdued and chastened; its ethos is clearly "Art for Art's sake" – a necessary sentiment if Wagner's music dramas are to be "rehabilitated."

56 Robert Layton, "Sibelius on Record," in *Sibelius Studies*, ed. Timothy L. Jackson and Veijo Murtomäki (Cambridge: Cambridge University Press, forthcoming).

57 For example, in *The Furtwängler Record*, John Ardoin never addresses the issue whether the "wartime" i.e. Nazi interpretations have political and morally reprehensible connotations. He simply asserts their qualitative superiority to most of the conductor's post-war efforts.

58 Bachmann, *Karajan*, p. 114.

59 Karajan recorded the Sixth Symphony frequently. Here are some of his representative timings for the March: in 1949, it was 8'13", in 1964 8'44", in 1972 8'12", and in 1985 8'29". Only the 1972 recording approaches the 1939 interpretation in electrifying intensity; indeed, musically the 1972 recording is far superior to the 1939 performance because Karajan now hears and brings out much more of Tchaikovsky's ingenious counterpoint, most of which was sacrificed for overall effect in the 1939 performance. Not only has Karajan learned much about the piece in the thirty-odd years separating the two recordings, the technique of orchestral playing has finally caught up with his demands.

60 Bachmann, *Karajan*, p. 123.

61 *Mengelberg Catalogue*, p. 158, item 251.

62 Bachmann, *Karajan*, p. 105.

63 George L. Mosse, *Fallen Soldiers: Reshaping the Memory of the World Wars* (New York: Oxford University Press, 1990), p. 90.

64 Friedrich Herzfeld, *Wilhelm Furtwängler. Weg und Wesen* (Leipzig: Wilhelm Goldmann Verlag, 1941), pp. 134–35.

65 The four Tchaikovsky films are: Carl Froehlich, *Es war eine rauschende Ballnacht* (Germany 1939), Glazer, *Song of My Heart* (USA 1948), Talankin, *Tchaikovsky* (USSR/USA 1970), and Ken Russell, *The Music Lovers* (Great Britain 1971).

Select bibliography

Editions and facsimiles

Tchaikovsky, Pyotr. *Symphony No. 6 in B Minor "Pathétique"* Op. 74 Full Score. Ed. Thomas Kohlhase (Mainz: Schott, 1993)

Sixth Symphony. Pathétique. Facsimile of the Full Score (Moscow: State Publishers, 1970), preface and commentary by Galina Pribegina

Sixth Symphony. Pathétique. Facsimile of the Sketches (Moscow: State Publishers, 1962)

Symphony in E flat. Completed, Scored, and Edited by Semyon Bogatyrev (Hamburg: Musikverlag Sikorski, 1961)

Books and articles

Ardoin, John. *The Furtwängler Record* (Portland: Amadeus Press, 1994)

Bachmann, Robert C. *Karajan. Notes on a Career*, trans. Shaun Whiteside (London: Quartet Books, 1990)

Barsova, Inna. "Mahler – ein Schüler Čajkovskijs?" in *Čajkovskij-Studien. Internationales Čajkovskij-Symposium Tübingen 1993*, ed. Thomas Kohlhase (Mainz: Schott, 1995), pp. 51–56

Berberova, Nina. "Looking Back at Tchaikovsky," trans. Vincent Giroud, *The Yale Review* 80 (1992), 60–73

Bertensson, Sergei and Jay Leyda. *Sergei Rachmaninoff. A Lifetime in Music* (New York: NYU Press, 1956)

Brown, David. *Tchaikovsky: A Biographical and Critical Study*, vol. I, *The Early Years (1840–1874)*, vol. II, *The Crisis Years (1874–1878)*, vol. III, *The Years of Wandering (1878–1885)*, vol. IV, *The Final Years (1885–1893)* (New York: Norton, 1976–91)

Tchaikovsky Remembered (London: Faber and Faber, 1993)

"How Did Tchaikovsky Come to Die – and Does It Really Matter?" Review-Article, *Music & Letters* 78 (1997), 581–88 (review of Alexander Poznansky's *Tchaikovsky's Last Days: a Documentary Study*)

Cooper, Martin. "The Symphonies," in *The Music of Tchaikovsky*, ed. Gerald Abraham (New York, 1946)

Dennis, David B. *Beethoven in German Politics 1870–1989* (New Haven: Yale University Press, 1996)

Garden, Edward. *Tchaikovsky* (London: J. M. Dent, 1973)

Greenberg, David. *The Construction of Homosexuality* (Chicago: University of Chicago Press, 1991)

Hepokoski, James. "Fiery-Pulsed Libertine or Domestic Hero? Strauss's *Don Juan*, Revisited," in *Richard Strauss. New Perspectives on the Composer and His Work*, ed. Bryan Gilliam (Durham: Duke University Press, 1992) pp. 135–76

Sibelius: Symphony No. 5 (Cambridge: Cambridge University Press, 1993)

Holden, Anthony. *Tchaikovsky* (London: Penguin Books, 1997)

Jackson, Timothy L. "Aspects of Sexuality and Structure in the Later Symphonies of Tchaikovsky," *Music Analysis* 14 (1995), 3–25

"The Finale of Bruckner's Seventh Symphony and Tragic Reversed Sonata Form," in *Bruckner Studies*, ed. Timothy L. Jackson and Paul Hawkshaw (Cambridge: Cambridge University Press, 1997), pp. 140–208

"The Meta-*Ursatz*, Crystallization, and Entropy in Jean Sibelius," in *Sibelius Studies*, ed. Timothy L. Jackson and Veijo Murtomäki (Cambridge: Cambridge University Press, forthcoming)

Karlinsky, Simon. "Should We Retire Tchaikovsky?" *Christopher Street*, May 1988, pp. 20–21

"Man or Myth? The Retrieval of the True Tchaikovsky," *Times Literary Supplement*, 17 January 1992

Kearney, Leslie, ed. *Tchaikovsky and His World* (Princeton: Princeton University Press, 1998)

Kendall, Alan. *Tchaikovsky: A Biography* (London: Bodley Head, 1988)

Kholopov, Yuri. "On the System of Musical Forms in the Symphonies of Tchaikovsky," *Sovetskaya Muzyka* 1990/6, 38–45

Kraus, Joseph C. "Tonal Plan and Narrative Plot in Tchaikovsky's Symphony No. 5 in E Minor," *Music Theory Spectrum* 13 (1991), 21–47

"The 'Russian' Influence in the First Symphony of Jean Sibelius: Chance Intersection or Profound Integration?," *Conference Report of the Second International Sibelius Conference in Helsinki, November 1995*, ed. Veijo Murtomäki, Kari Kilpeläinen and Risto Väisänen (Helsinki: Sibelius Academy, 1998), pp. 142–52

"Tchaikovsky," in *The Nineteenth Century Symphony*, ed. D. Kern Holoman (New York: Schirmer Books, 1997), pp. 299–326

Locke, Ralph P. "Constructing the Oriental 'Other': Saint-Saens's *Samson et Dalila,*" *Cambridge Opera Journal* 3 (1991), 261–302

Martyn, Barrie. *Rachmaninoff. Composer, Pianist, Conductor* (London: Scolar Press, 1990)

McClary, Susan. *Feminine Endings: Music, Gender and Sexuality* (University of Minnesota Press, 1991)

    Georges Bizet, Carmen (Cambridge: Cambridge University Press, 1992)

Orlova, Alexandra. "Tchaikovsky: The Last Chapter," *Music and Letters* 62 (1981), 125–45

    Tchaikovsky: A Self-Portrait (Oxford: Oxford University Press, 1990)

Poznansky, Alexander. "Tchaikovsky's Suicide: Myth and Reality," *19th-Century Music* 11 (1988), 199–220

    Tchaikovsky: The Quest for the Inner Man (New York: Schirmer, 1991)

    Tchaikovsky's Last Days (Oxford: Oxford University Press, 1996)

    "Tchaikovsky: A Life Reconsidered," in *Tchaikovsky and His World*, ed. Kearney, pp. 3–54

Pribegina, Galina A. "Tchaikovsky's Sixth Symphony (Based on the Manuscript Materials)," in *Iz istorii russkoi i sovetskoi muzyki* (*From the History of Russian and Soviet Music*), vol. II, ed. Aleksei Kandiniskii and Juliya Rozanova (Moscow, 1976)

Prieberg, Fred K. *Musik im NS-Staat.* (Frankfurt: Fischer, 1982)

    "Furtwängler: Repräsentant oder Saboteur?" in *Wilhelm Furtwängler in Diskussion. Sieben Beiträge* ed. Chris Walton (Winterthur: Amadeus Verlag, 1996), pp. 65–74

    Kraftprobe: Wilhelm Furtwängler im Dritten Reich (Wiesbaden: Brockhaus, 1986)

Seibert, Donald C. "The Tchaikovsky Fifth: A Symphony without a Program," *Music Review* 51 (1990), 36–45

Sokolov, Valery Solomonovish. "Do i posle tragedii" ("Before and After the Tragedy"), in Nicolai Blinov, *Posledniaia bolezn'i smert' P. I. Chaikovskogo* (*The Last Illness and Death of Tchaikovsky*) (Moscow, 1994), pp. 136–203

    Antonina Chaikovskaia: istoriia zabytoi zhizni (*Antonina Chaikovskaia: the History of a Forgotten Life*) (Moscow, 1994)

Taruskin, Richard. "Tchaikovsky, Fallen from Grace," *The New York Times*, 30 June 1991

    "Pathetic Symphonist. Chaikovsky, Russia, Sexuality and the Study of Music," *The New Republic*, 6 February 1995

Tchaikovsky, Modest I. *Zhizn P. I. Chaikovskogo* (*The Life of P. I. Tchaikovsky*), 3 vols. (Moscow, 1900–02). Abridged and translated by Rosa Newmarch in

The Life and Letters of Peter Ilich Tchaikovsky by Modeste Tchaikovsky (London, 1903)

Tchaikovsky, Pyotr I. *Polnoye sobraniye sochineny: literaturnye proizvidenia i perepiska* (*Complete edition: Literary works and correspondence*), 17 vols. (Moscow, 1953–81)

Vaidman, Polina. "Unbekannter Čajkovskij – Entwürfe zu nicht ausgeführten Kompositionen," in *Čajkovskij-Studien. Internationales Čajkovskij-Symposium Tübingen 1993*, ed. Thomas Kohlhase (Mainz: Schott, 1995), pp. 281–91

Vaidman, P. E. and G. I. Belonovich, eds. *P. I. Chaikovskii: zabytoe i novoe, vospominaniia sovremennikov, novye materialy i dokumenty* (*P. I. Tchaikovsky: Forgotten and New Reminiscences of Contemporaries, New Materials and Documents*) (Moscow, 1995)

Volkov, Solomon. *Balanchine's Tchaikovsky* (New York: Simon and Schuster, 1985)

A Cultural History of St. Petersburg trans. Antonina W. Bouis (New York: The Free Press, 1996)

Walton, Chris. *Wilhelm Furtwängler in Diskussion. Sieben Beiträge* (Winterthur: Amadeus Verlag, 1996)

Warrack, John. *Tchaikovsky. Symphonies and Concertos* (London: British Broadcasting Corporation, 1969)

Tchaikovsky. Ballet Music (London: British Broadcasting Corporation, 1979)

Tchaikovsky (London: Hamish Hamilton, 1989)

Wiley, Roland. *Tchaikovsky's Ballets* (Oxford: Oxford University Press, 1991)

Zajaczkowski, Henry. "Tchaikovsky's Fourth Symphony," *Music Review* 45 (1984), 265–76

Tchaikovsky's Musical Style (Ann Arbor: UMI Research Press, 1987)

Index